Leslie,
You've Got This!
Vicki Gustafson.

Sgt. Jay Gustafson
0548

Endorsements

"*His Badge, My Story* is a must-read for spouses of law enforcement officers. It captures every emotion, fear, and insecurity harbored by those who love and support men in blue and does it with grace, strength, humor, and a quiet dignity. It is hard for any of us to put into words the range of feelings we have about sending spouses out into the world each day, knowing that they have an obligation to protect and serve others besides us and may not come home. Vicki Gustafson reminds us that it is a special calling that beckons us—not just our spouses—to be quiet warriors and supporters and to be a glue that holds things together. Yes, there are huge sacrifices, but there is an honor in our calling and a strength that we can find, in each other and God, to serve in the very special role that has been bestowed upon us. I thank Vicki for putting her story and some very raw emotions out there to help us all ponder our sacrifices and to remind us of the pride we should feel about supporting men in blue."

Judge Stacey G.C. Jernigan
Law Enforcement Officer's Wife
Irving, Texas

"During my 20-year-long career as a criminologist working with law enforcement across the United States, I have come to learn of the hard realities experienced by families in the law enforcement community. The sacrifice of the men and women in uniform who, on a daily basis, risk their lives to save others, does not go unnoticed. However, the silent heroes are those that support them and are often at home with a prayer book at hand, asking God to bring them home safely. I refer to them as being 'silent' since we seldom hear about them.

"Thanks to Vicki Gustafson, the term *silent* will no longer apply to those courageous families that support men and women in blue. In her book, *His Badge, My Story,* you will find the inspiration, stories, and support that many of these families need and have shared with each other over the years. I endorse this book and strongly recommend that you read it in order to understand their hard realities. It will be then that we will no longer refer to these families as being silent but instead call them 'heroes'—a title they all deserve!"

Alex del Carmen, Ph.D.
Criminologist
Arlington, Texas

"There are few who are in a better position to support the spouses of law enforcement officers than Vicki. After forty years of being married to a man who wore the badge, raising a family, and living out a career as a woman who built life on faith and family, her words will surely be a gift to thousands of women who are in the throes of figuring out what it is to partner with a man in the shared mutual sacrifices of this unique calling."

Reverend Mike Ramsdell
Mansfield, Texas

"*His Badge, My Story* is an inspirational book that reminds law enforcement officer families of the importance of relying on God to strengthen marriages. While reading this book, my wife and I were able to relate to many of the chapters. It gave us a sense of comfort knowing we are not alone in some of the challenges we have faced. This book was an amazing tool to help us both understand the value of faith, communication, and support in our daily lives. I highly recommend it to any couple looking for encouragement and insight on how to build a successful marriage while facing challenges that the law enforcement life may bring about."

Sergeant Travis Waybourn
Mansfield Police Department
Burleson, Texas

"Vicki is not only a compassionate writer and law enforcement officer's wife. She is also a gifted entrepreneur, business leader, and life coach who generously uses her lifetime of experiences to mentor, lead, and coach others through life's challenges and opportunities with her signature common-sense style."

Beth Jones-Schall
Spirit of Success, Inc.
Cranberry Township, Pennsylvania

"A compassionate heart, an inquisitive mind, and a desire to serve well are qualities I would look for in a coaching relationship. Vicki Gustafson is a tireless learner and has so much to share. The women she serves can be assured that she has been there and felt the highs and lows of a law enforcement spouse and mother. How fortunate that she has set these into writing in such a compelling way!"

Anne Hunter
Cabi Co-Founder
Edina, Minnesota

"Many local heroes go unnoticed. Perhaps the spouses and families of all hero law enforcement officers should be recognized. It has been my privilege to know Vicki and Jay Gustafson and their loving family for over thirty years. We met when our children were in preschool and Jay had relatively few years behind his badge. It became evident very quickly that this was a very dedicated and loving family, and that law enforcement was a major calling in all of their lives. I can recall many stories and events and late-night phone call discussions, many of which have culminated in this wonderful book. Vicki began making contributions toward understanding law enforcement wives by being one and living the unique experiences. She continues to contribute many years later with sharing those poignant experiences in the publication of this beneficial book.

"Having known her personally, I can say she is a person who leads by example and inspires others by her dedication, her faith, her love of family, and her strong work ethic. She is kind, generous, and a dynamic person. Her adaptability to situations makes her an excellent leader and coach. I have appreciated her conviction and integrity in situations in the past. I am confident that her words and experiences will help readers to act courageously and give them clear insight to the unique and noble experience of being an integral part of a law enforcement family."

Teri Anton
Dalworthington Gardens, Texas

"*His Badge, My Story* takes the stress, struggles, and firsthand experiences of being married to a law enforcement officer and shares them as a journey of inspiration, faith, and love. As the wife of a police officer, I think this book will be helpful to some, comforting to others, and life-changing for still more."

Carrie Velder
High School Principal (Assistant Principal)
Law Enforcement Officers Wife
Midlothian, Texas

"As the wife of a retired Secret Service agent and now the mother of a Lexington, Kentucky, police officer, I found *His Badge, My Story* an inspiration for LEO families across the nation.

"Vicki incorporates her life experiences in combination with her Christian faith into a concise book that serves as both a relevant and inspiring aid for law enforcement spouses to better understand their husband, their career path, and the nature of police work itself.

"I found Vicki's insightful perspective extremely relatable and comforting to the situations and adversities I have faced as the wife of a law enforcement officer and continue to face as a mother of a law enforcement officer."

Andrea Hazlewood
Crestwood Kentucky
Wife of retired Secret Service agent and mother of Lexington, Kentucky, police officer

HIS BADGE, *My Story*

Insights for Spouses and Loved Ones of
Law Enforcement Officers

VICKI GUSTAFSON

WESTBOW
PRESS®

A DIVISION OF THOMAS NELSON
& ZONDERVAN

WestBow Press books may be ordered through booksellers or by contacting:

WestBow Press
A Division of Thomas Nelson & Zondervan
1663 Liberty Drive
Bloomington, IN 47403
www.westbowpress.com
1 (866) 928-1240

ISBN: 978-1-9736-4750-8 (sc)
ISBN: 978-1-9736-4749-2 (hc)
ISBN: 978-1-9736-4751-5 (e)

Library of Congress Control Number: 2018914336

Printed in the United States of America.

WestBow Press rev. date: 04/03/2019

DEDICATION

I DEDICATE THIS BOOK TO my strong and courageous husband and daughter.

To my beautiful daughter, I pray you keep the faith through your journey as a wife of a police officer. Be armed with the love of God and your imaginary bulletproof vest. Be patient and understanding and most importantly, enjoy life together. You've got this! Love you to the moon and back.

To my personal hero and husband, Jay, who supported and encouraged me to complete this book. Thank you for allowing me to share my story because of your badge and for sharing your expertise and experiences in law enforcement. I pray you always stay safe. My love forever.

CONTENTS

FOREWORD

I HAVE ALWAYS STOOD IN awe at the incredible men and women who serve in law enforcement. Bravery is certainly a required attribute, but willingness to sacrifice may be even more critical. Every man and woman behind the badge that I have interviewed in my thirty-plus years in policing has told me they wanted to enter the profession so they could "help others." I've witnessed that narrative play out time and time again over the years as they did just that—helped and saved.

Early in my career, I worked as many as five concurrent off-duty jobs. I also went back to school and obtained two graduate degrees. And I sometimes made unpopular decisions that were met with negative and public reactions. While I was always aware of the special gifts all cops seem to have, I didn't always appreciate the fact that someone who loved me "held my ladder" as I matriculated across police department assignments and climbed the command hierarchy.

The path of policing, whether on the street or in the office, sometimes requires venturing into unfamiliar and "hostile" territory. I managed to survive the physical trauma, but the mental and emotional tolls mounted. I came to see, through all my years of service, that it was my wife who was there "holding my ladder." She held it when I felt like I was about to falter, and she helped me get back on whatever rung that collapsed under me. She did all of it while giving birth to and raising our three wonderful young people: one now a medical doctor, another a licensed professional counselor, and the baby who is determined to save the world between now and graduating from the University of Texas.

My career and family success are in large measure due to my wife's support. I had thousands of hours of police training classes to teach me tactics, operations, supervision, leadership, and management. I had so much support from coworkers and community members. But the one person for whom no success template existed until now is my hero, friend, and wife, Denise.

Vicki Gustafson, through her own dedicated, loving, and selfless experience, has created a masterpiece. *His Badge, My Story* offers readers what I didn't know how to give to my incredible spouse. Thanks to Vicki, the guide that Denise didn't have during my years of service is available to those hundreds of thousands of police spouses, significant others, and family members.

This incredible work gives insight into the life of a law enforcement officer and equips loved ones to live with and support their officer. Its reader-friendly format invites you into each chapter with real-life experiences, and it offers proven suggestions for coping with those inevitable policing challenges.

Vicki Gustafson, through this book, has now made it possible for us to hold the ladder for law enforcement spouses, significant others, and family members who love and support them.

Theron L. Bowman, Ph.D.
Chief of Police and Deputy City Manager (Retired)
Arlington, Texas

PREFACE

HIS BADGE, MY STORY has been a labor of love. My desire to make a difference for law enforcement officers (LEO) couples is what encouraged me to complete this book. The more insight and understanding loved ones have, the better the chances these couples will enjoy a long, happy life together.

This book is for spouses of law enforcement officers. However what it covers extends to significant others: parents, friends, and all loved ones. All readers will gain insight into the life and unique challenges and struggles officers and their families may experience.

For simplicity and consistency I will refer to all loved ones as LEOW's, which stands for Law Enforcement Officers Wives.

His Badge, My Story touches on issues I believe are common to LEO families, including communication, worry and fear, the pitfalls of their career, and the struggles of scheduling and balancing the career with family life and life in society. Other topics such as sacrifices and raising children are ones most LEOWs can relate to as well.

The approach of taking a specific topic, such as worry and fear, and sharing my experiences with it, I believe, creates a relatable story. I was vulnerable and authentic to offer readers an "inside" look at each situation presented.

For thirty-eight years of our forty-year marriage, my husband, Jay and I have worked through challenges, struggles, and emotions—and the journey continues. I'm now experiencing how it feels to have a daughter married to a law enforcement officer.

My first step in preparing the material in this book was to reach out to a few friends in law enforcement who I trusted with the idea of sharing my experiences. I created a questionnaire and used it to stay focused and on task. One of my first interviews was with Harold Elliott, a chaplain for the Arlington Police Department in Texas. The moment I stepped into his home, before we could even sit down, he challenged me.

"Tell them something they don't already know," he said. "They know about shift work, the danger, the underpaid and overworked officers. They have heard about pitfalls, isolation, and more."

His words were thought provoking! Harold's challenge became the framework of *His Badge, My Story.*

Each chapter begins with a BOLO (be on the lookout), a sneak peek of what is to come. Many chapters contain real-life police stories that my husband and I faced during his twenty-six years with the Arlington Police Department (APD) in Texas. I share insights and challenges from my perspective.

At the end of each chapter, a Debriefing section summarizes the BOLO message, provides hope and resolutions to stories, and offers suggested resources for your use. The Bullet Points portion of the Debriefing gives you "ammunition" to focus your thoughts on the chapter's topic, coping skills, and suggestions for further exploration. The Debriefing section also includes Scripture verses to reflect on.

This book becomes increasingly more compelling because it includes stories from the lives of many other LEOs and LEOWs. Their contributions take this book from good to great.

As you travel through this book, you will notice I talk openly about my faith. Your faith journey will be unique to you. My hope is that you will reflect on your belief.

It has been a fun and challenging three years to complete this project. Holding the published book in my hands and knowing you are doing the same is an accomplishment Jay and I are very proud of.

ACKNOWLEDGMENTS

B E ON THE LOOKOUT for amazing people who helped make *His Badge, My Story* remarkable! Their words of wisdom, insight, and willingness to be a part of this incredible book are a blessing to me and all who read it.

A deep appreciation goes to my editors and publisher; they saw my vision and shaped my concept. A special thank you to Karen Roberts, my brilliant editor with RQuest, LLC. I am so glad Karen likes working with first-time writers; she patiently taught me how to become an "official" author. To Libby Hanaway, your expertise with the poem was greatly appreciated. And to my publisher, WestBow Press, who has given me the platform to allow my passion to be heard among a wide audience of readers.

Thank you to all the wonderful people who kindly endorsed *His Badge, My Story*: Teri Anton; Alex del Carmen, Ph.D.; Judge Stacey Jernigan; Andrea Hazlewood; Anne Hunter; Reverend Mike Ramsdell; Beth Jones-Schall; Carrie Velder; and Sergeant Travis Waybourn. And a special thank you to Retired Chief Theron Bowman, Ph.D., for supporting this book with an exceptional Foreword.

Thank you Kristen Gustafson with Poshlings Photography for capturing Jay's and my smile and heart through your lens.

To my family, all my encouragers, and special people, I am so very grateful: Reverend Sarah Allen, Barbara Eggiman, Sara Grady, Trisha Goode, Angela Pritchett, Robin Pou, Katie Robbins, and Sammie Slocum.

I would like to thank God for giving me the strength, courage and wisdom. Without His guidance and blessings, this book would not have been possible.

Finally, my heartfelt thank you goes to all the additional officers, their spouses, and family members for their stories and words of wisdom. We are fortunate to read and learn from the experiences of these individuals: Maria Barreda-Alvarado, PJ Brock and Mark Price, Wendy and Clint Burgess, Brittany Cook, Jeri Lyn Crocker, Chaplain Harold Elliott, Jessica and Houston Gass, Caroline and Michael Gresham, Dick Hill, Allan Hudson, JoAnne and Robert Lane, Theresa Lozada, Don Pilcher, Janis and Denny Proffitt, Mary and Gary Shipp, Janet and Billy Seals, Marcie Schneider, Kimberley and Jimmy Salinas, Cassidy and Travis Waybourn, Sarah and Grant Williams and Bryan Woodard.

INTRODUCTION

O N AUGUST 28, 2015, a uniformed officer was shot to death "execution style" in broad daylight while pumping gas. This horrific murder was a deliberate killing, and it happened in the state where I live.

Words cannot describe the sadness I felt for the officer's family. I could only imagine what his wife and children would have to go through. Law enforcement officers' families across the country mourned the loss, while most of the country just watched the news and sighed. Some must have said, "Oh, how sad." Unfortunately, a few silently applauded, idolizing the shooter.

That afternoon I received a phone call from JoAnne, a young, new police wife. It was Robert, her husband's first day to work solo. He'd been "cut loose," as my husband calls it, which is his slang for describing the day a rookie officer goes out on his own after completing his time with a training officer.

I heard and felt the concern in JoAnne's voice over the phone.

"Did you hear the news about the deputy shooting?" she asked in an almost panicked tone. "He was shot and killed, and all he was doing was pumping gas!

What do I do? How do I handle this?"

My heart sank. Quickly I gathered my thoughts, and then I realized how important it was to share with JoAnne how I personally learned to cope with these tragic events. I know her well. She's a pretty tough gal and would have seen right through a sugarcoated response.

"Pray for his family and your husband," I said calmly, "and turn off the news. Limit your time on social media right now to avoid hearing more about this offense." And then I added my own one-liner, bluntly: "JoAnne, get used to it."

The deep breath she took was audible.

"Yes, it's heartbreaking," I said. "Your compassion for the loss is understandable and deserved. However, it is important for your well-being to develop coping skills to manage the tragedies in the weekly news. If you don't, they could tear you up inside."

JoAnne agreed but went on to say, "I can't just put my head in the sand. The news is everywhere!"

I held my tongue but thought silently, *My head is never in the sand.*

JoAnne was right. It seems impossible for police wives to bury their heads in the sand. They and their families are bombarded regularly with news like this story, especially on social media.

When my conversation with JoAnne ended, it was my turn to take a deep breath, say a prayer for this young LEOW and her husband, say another prayer for the fallen officer's family, and then shed a silent tear.

That day JoAnne and Robert experienced the reality of losing a family member in our Blue Nation. I imagined the steps Robert would take, as he was about to begin his first solo shift. He would take a deep breath, set his thoughts aside, put on his vest and uniform, and prepare himself emotionally to go to work. I visualized JoAnne, in silence, closely watching Robert as he wrapped his badge with a black band, as he had been taught, to show his feeling of loss and to honor the fallen officer.

I imagined, in that moment, JoAnne's own invisible bulletproof vest beginning to form. It would protect her in the same way his actual vest protected him.

You may not have picked up on it, but I don't watch the news very often. That day, however, I wanted to know more. I was disturbed by the way the media addressed the officer's murder so matter-of-factly. Also, I was shocked by how American society, for the most part, didn't understand how the loss of a public servant could affect the community. My heart was heavy, and after the conversation with JoAnne, I felt the need to do something. But what?

How can I make a difference? I thought to myself. *What can I do to help change the way society feels about police officers? Would it help law enforcement officer's wives like JoAnne if I shared my own experiences?*

Many years ago, I prepared a devotional for a Bible study class about what it was like to be married to a cop. The devotional was my response to the "The Law and Justice" Bible study guide the class was using to learn about the Old Testament stories of Moses and Joshua. When the time came, I presented my devotional to the class, which was a poem I entitled "Coffee and Donuts: A Tribute to My Husband."

The class members were amazed and surprised by what they heard. There wasn't a dry eye in the room. They encouraged me to share my poem with others and copyright it. At the time, the thought of sharing what I had written with others outside of that room was more than I was ready for.

"Coffee and Donuts: A Tribute to My Husband" has been on display in a hallway in my home for over twenty years. This year I was drawn to reread it, and I decided it was time for me to share it, along with my story as the wife of a police officer, with those who are experiencing life with a LEO as well. Like the people in Bible study when I first presented the poem, I thought others might appreciate it or want to get a better understanding of the people behind the badge and those who support them.

As you read *His Badge, My Story*, you'll feel my passion for life, family, God, and the pride I have for my husband. You'll encounter intense emotions, many times entangled together, including love, loneliness, honor, pride, sadness, fear, anxiety, compassion, and frustration.

If you haven't already, it won't be long before you experience your own "coffee and donuts" stories as well as the web of emotions and struggles because of his badge, "the calling" your husband answered.

More than likely you will face hardships. Be prepared to face them with strength, honor, and courage. Most importantly, however, you will experience what it feels like to live with a hero. A feeling of pride will rush over you like chills from a cool breeze on a hot summer day. And that pride will deepen the love in your heart for the law enforcement officer in your life. My prayer is that you will find hope and strength, with God's help, to overcome whatever challenges you face.

You can enjoy a lifetime of happiness with your officer even though you may hear the odds are against your marriage. Your life together is worth the fight. He needs you by his side. He needs your love, support, understanding, and lots of hugs—hugs he can feel all the way through his bulletproof vest. You need those hugs also, ones that enable you to feel his heart beating through the steel-like plate that protects him.

Keep in mind he will retire someday. When the two of you look back, you can say, together, "We did it. Job well done! We made it through the thrilling, roller- coaster ride in the world of law enforcement."

So pull up a chair and get comfortable. It's time for me to share our "coffee and donuts" stories.

COFFEE AND DONUTS
A Tribute to My Husband

I've been asked quite often over the past twenty years,
"Don't you worry about him or have any fears?"
It's not the whole truth, but I'll say with a smile,
"Oh, he takes care of himself, no reason to worry.
It's just coffee and donuts," I add in a hurry.
Then I close my eyes briefly to hold back a tear,
And say a quick prayer for the cops far and near.

As a rookie, he's so excited! But this isn't pretend,
Crime really does exist in this land.
He's strapped on a gun, a badge, courage, and more,
But I see he's forgotten his vest on the floor.
Should I worry? Not me! You've got to be kidding.
It's just coffee and donuts—*oh, how fitting.*

He's changed quite a bit as the years have gone by.
In a crowd, his arms are crossed as he stands alone in a corner.
I think to myself, *Can I live with this man?*

At times he's bitter and frustrated, and I don't understand.
Then God quietly reminds me of His ultimate plan.

The next thing I know, he walks through the door
With a rose in his hand, and he wants to say more.
He tells me he's sorry he's been acting this way,
Last week he was challenged in a dangerous way.
I was afraid to hear it, so I quickly turned away,
Walked into my room and began to pray.

As our children were born, he started to see
This vest was important for them and for me.
Patrol came and went, close calls and arrests.
He's got a new assignment—Yes! Now I can rest!
Coffee and donuts? I should buy extra this time.
He has an eight-to-five job to investigate crimes.

His uniform now stored, he proceeds to get dressed.
I watch him get ready, and he says, "No need for my vest."
But the next thing I know, I see photos of him,
Carrying dead bodies from where someone has sinned.

My heart skips a beat 'cause I know what is next.
He's worked really hard, and he's done very his best.
Then we sit in the courtroom and listen to this—
A lawyer turns with a vengeance to say,
"This man's done no wrong, it's the officer at fault.
He's jumped to conclusions, so let this man walk!"

With God by his side, justice prevails.
The man is found guilty of murder and is sentenced to jail.
Then we go home, but we cannot sleep.
Oh, it's just coffee and donuts—*that's what some people think!*

On certain nights he tosses and turns, then wakes in a cold sweat,
This time he's remembering the infant just laid to rest.
Killed by his own father's hands—no remorse, just a grin.
The man was set free and walked away from his sin.
"Where's the justice in this?" my husband would say.
Then I reminded him in God's time, it will happen one day.

One evening he tells me as he takes off his vest,
How he went inside, gun drawn—but after the rest.
SWAT had knocked open the door, just like on TV,
And my heart was pounding as he told this to me.
Though I never let on how I worried inside,
Oh, those coffee and donuts! I'd think with a sigh.

He moved, once again, to an undercover job
And traded his vest for a slick car and suit.
"Oh, no need to worry, honey. It's just prostitutes!"
That's right, I'd tell myself, *there's nothing to fear,*
Just strippers and dopers and cop haters there.
It's the law of the land he's asked to control,
Same as Moses and Joshua, or so I've been told.

He calls me one sunny morning and says,
"The perverts are back in the park today,
And to think I arrested them just yesterday."
Disappointing the kids, I put the picnic basket away.
I tell them their dad said the park is too crowded again,
As he tries to shelter our kids from these terrible sins.

Assignment change back to patrol, and it frightens me so.
He's armed with a cross in his pocket, a badge, gun, and vest,
But these sturdy protections give me very little rest.
Once again he walks out the door, dressed like a cop.
With the "Cop Killer" song popular, I feel my heart drop.

Where does it come from, the courage, the nerve,
To continue to go out, to protect and to serve?
I bet if you ask him, he'd smile with a wink,
"From *The Wizard of Oz*, of course!
What else could you think?"

I tell everyone—himself and me too—
"Oh, I'm used to this now, there's nothing to do.
I'll get away from it all and watch some TV."
But when I flip through the channels, what do I see?
A rerun of him on *Unsolved Mysteries*!
It's been twenty years of coffee and donuts, you see,
As he proceeds to go out to protect you and me.

I was reminded last week of the death of two cops,
Killed by a drunk driver—and I think my heart stopped.
I couldn't read about them, it bothered me so,
That their families are without them
Yet their children would still grow.

As I walked away with tears down my cheek,
I shuddered to think, *Could this happen to him?*
It wasn't just coffee and donuts for them.
And now our hearts slowly mend.

Next time you see him, arms crossed in the crowd,
All alone in a corner he will stand.
Oh, it took me a while, but with God's help I now understand,
And I'm proud to say, "I live with this man."
He's not alone; he's with God, hand in hand.
It's just natural for him to stand apart and watch over us,
Twenty years of experience, I don't put up a fuss.

I love this cop dearly and want him to know
God and I are by his side daily, wherever he goes.

My prayers are changing with each passing year,
And I'll still privately battle with worry and fear.
God bless this man and his chosen career!

With law and justice, it's all still the same,
Just twisted a little as each year came.
They still serve coffee and donuts,
And he's saved up a few.
He'll share them someday with me and with you.

Vicki Gustafson ©1996, 2018

BOLO 1

Impressionable Minds

Be on the lookout (in retrospect) for indications throughout your husband's past to help you understand his desire to become a law enforcement officer. The television shows he watched or the sports he was involved in could have influenced his life and led him to become a law enforcement officer. He also may have had an officer in his life who served as a role model to his young, impressionable mind.

J AY GUSTAFSON WAS RAISED in a family of proud Americans, and as it so happened, he was born on Veterans Day, November 11. As a young child, his kindhearted and loving mother, Argie, would take him to her workplace so they could watch the annual Veterans Day parade together. She was a bookkeeper, and her office was on the eleventh floor of a building in downtown Fort Worth, Texas. It was the perfect viewing spot for the parade.

Jay remembers seeing flags waving, veterans, bands marching, and citizens cheering. His impressionable mind, as a young child, thought it was "pretty special." More importantly, for the first few years as he watched the parade, he thought all these festivities were in celebration of his birthday!

Jay's father, James, was a disabled American veteran (DAV) from World War II. Jay was proud to be his only son. After the war, his father opened his own barbershop and worked tirelessly until his health restricted him from working long hours on his feet. By the time I met Jay's parents, his mother was working from home so she could be the caregiver for Jay's dad.

When Jay was eight years old, his sister, Janis (who is ten years older), married Denny Proffitt, a law enforcement officer sixteen years older than Jay. He couldn't help but look up to Denny. His stature alone required it. This gentle giant of a man was extremely impressive to Jay, especially when he was in uniform.

In his deep voice, Denny would often tell Jay police stories about cases he worked on. Jay would sit wide-eyed, soaking in every word. In hindsight, even then Jay's choices foreshadowed his later career choice in law enforcement. He was a proud crossing guard and a hall monitor at his elementary school, and he mindfully portrayed himself as being in his brother-in-law's world. It was no surprise to the family that the law enforcement television shows *Dragnet*, *Adam 12*, and *Starsky and Hutch* were among his favorite weekly programs.

Jay enjoyed school and was elected class president in the ninth grade at William James Jr. High, a leadership role he was proud of. He also loved playing sports, especially baseball and football, and he excelled in both. His parents went to every game and watched him as he played linebacker on defense and center for offense. His efforts earned him a letter in football during his ninth grade in junior high, which was a big deal. In his sophomore year at Poly High School, Jay lettered again, another big deal in the world of sports.

Because he loved baseball as well, Jay and his family traveled to different little league baseball tournaments and later to high school tournaments. His mom and dad enjoyed watching their son play third base.

Jay learned a lot from being active in sports. His life lessons included skills, discipline, teamwork, leadership, responsibility, and the value of hard work. He also learned to practice hard, play hard, obey the rules, and have fun. All of these behaviors are traits a law enforcement officer needs to perform his duties.

Life lessons are also learned through experiences, which sometimes are out of one's own control. Jay was a happy-go-lucky teenager with lots of friends; however, right before his junior year in high school, his parents moved to an apartment on the opposite side of town. Jay had to transfer from Poly High to the brand-new Southwest High School. He wasn't happy about leaving his childhood friends behind, but deep down, he knew it was the right move for everyone.

It wasn't easy at first. Jay had to adjust to his new environment, find new friends, and push himself even harder to continue to excel in baseball and football. His outgoing, fun personality allowed him to make new friends quickly, and his new coaches were thrilled to have him. Unfortunately, because he had played varsity football for Poly High, he wasn't allowed to play varsity at Southwest High School. He had to accept the disappointment and play for the junior varsity team. During the adjustment phase, his mother would frequently remind him of her favorite saying. "Jay, you will just have to get happy in the same shoes you got mad in." I eventually adopted this saying and told it to our children when they were disappointed.

I tell you all this because a major event was about to occur, and it would literally knock Jay off his feet.

In Jay's senior year, his dream of playing varsity football and lettering for Southwest High was about to become a reality. He'd worked hard and played hard for years to reach this goal. He was at the top of his game and ready to tackle anything that came across his path. And then it happened.

During a preseason game against Poly High School, he became a target of revenge. One intentional bad clip behind Jay's knee, and—*boom!*—he went down for the count. His knee was shattered, along with his dream and opportunity to play and letter in varsity football for Southwest High School. He spent most of his senior year on the sidelines, healing from surgery and facing the painful experience of physical therapy. During this tough time, Jay learned how to accept his situation and face it with endurance and strength.

Jay was active in his church MYF (Methodist Youth Fellowship) as a young teenager. When the family moved to the southwest area of Fort Worth, Jay joined Young Life. He enjoyed attending its weekly meetings and annual camps. They helped strengthen his impressionable mind and relationship with God.

After graduation, which was a proud moment, Jay's parents encouraged him to attend the University of Texas at Arlington (UTA) to pursue a degree in business. "A business degree will open a lot of doors for you, son," his dad said. Jay took his parents' advice and was accepted at UTA. He played baseball and flag football for intramural sports teams. During the summer months, he worked at the Texas Highway Department.

Some roads we take in life will twist and turn, and if we stay on the wrong road long enough, it will eventually reach a dead end. After a few years of studies and a low interest in the field of business, Jay moved back home to rethink his direction. His parents helped him get a job working with a concrete company. His sister, Janis, and brother-in-law, Denny, would swing by from time to time to visit. Denny was sheriff of Bosque County, Texas, and Jay jumped at the chance to listen to him share his police stories again and again—as Denny had done when Jay was a young boy.

Not long after Jay's twenty-first birthday, he came face-to-face with another life lesson as he and two friends were returning home from a night out on the town. Jay was driving his 1970 Ford Mustang, Mach One, the car he had adored since high school. It had a burnt orange body with a black racing stripe down the middle—a very cool car back in the day! But after a brake failure, a hard turn, and a curb, the Mach One Mustang was done for. The car flipped and landed upside down in a ditch. By the grace of God, nobody was hurt, but his Mustang was totaled.

Once again Jay was devastated. There he was, twenty-one years old, with no car and living at home. Not a good combination.

Now what? I can't live at home forever, and this Monday–Friday, eight-to-five job is just a paycheck. Jay wondered. *What next? Where do I go from here?* He asked himself, *What is God's plan for me?*

Debriefing

It's interesting to look back on the journey we take in life. Where we came from. Where we went. How we got to where we are today. And what our impressionable minds picked up along the way.

Jay's brother-in-law, Denny, was the one person who towered above the rest in Jay's growing up years.

When I asked a handful of police officers why they chose this career, one said he became a police cadet because he'd heard the pay was fair and the work was flexible around his college schedule. Another said once he'd experienced what it was like to ride in a patrol car with a cop. It was a simple decision for him when he became of age.

Robert, JoAnne's husband, said, "I'm really not sure. I grew up around an air force base, so I saw a lot of guys in uniform. My father worked with and was friends with the police and fire chiefs. I guess I was comfortable around them."

The common thread I picked up on during all these interviews, however, was the statement that as a child, many of them didn't like to be in trouble. They liked to follow the rules. Some of them said it was the motivating factor—an excellent attribute for entering the field of law enforcement.

I believe God uses the people and situations in our lives to prepare us for our journeys ahead. In Jay's case, Denny was his role model, the one God placed on Jay's heart to pay extra attention to. His experiences in sports, Young Life, and his church youth group also prepared him to become the man he is today.

Bullet Points ===============

Consider asking your spouse the following questions, and then share with each other your life experiences that led you both to where you are today. It will be a fascinating story. I'm sure of it. Everyone has a story to tell. Both of your stories are equally important.

- What significant childhood experiences did your husband have while growing up?
- Was there someone in your husband's life as well that made an impression on him that might have contributed to his decision to become a police officer?
- How did they prepare him for his journey?
- How did your childhood experiences prepare you as a law enforcement officers wife?

Colossians 2:6–7 says, "So then, just as you received Christ Jesus as Lord, continue to live your lives in him, rooted and built up in him, strengthened in the faith as you were taught, and overflowing with thankfulness."

BOLO 2

"In Pursuit" of Love and Happiness

Be on the lookout for dreams that could come true! We all have to pursue our own dreams, not the dreams others have for us. Jay's dream was bold and daring. It included bright flashing lights and sirens. My dream was to find my soul mate, marry and have children. If I had to work, then I wanted to be my own boss.

I WAS BLESSED WITH WONDERFUL and loving parents. My father, Tom, was a generous man with a huge heart. He never raised his voice or said a curse word when he was upset, and we certainly didn't have guns in the house. Dad was a successful business owner of a local car dealership. Many these days would say he was "a product of his generation, a workaholic."

My mom, Joy, was a petite, four-foot-eleven-inch, stay-at-home, "energizer bunny". She may have been small in stature and in some ways frail, but she was tough as nails on the inside. Later in life, one of her memorable quotes I chuckled at was, "I'm a tough old bird, and you wouldn't want me for Thanksgiving!" Very appropriate statement coming from her. It was common to find her singing while she was baking in the kitchen. Mom was an excellent baker and she was willing to share her expertise with anyone who asked.

Mom was also known for her one-liner, encouraging words of wisdom. As an example, whenever I'd say, "I can't do …," she'd be quick to reply, saying, *"Can't* never could do nothin'," meaning my complaints of not being able to accomplish something were falling on deaf ears. She'd also say to me, "Vicki, you can do anything you put your mind to" and then add a little chaser, "Some things you *might* have to work harder at than others, but you can still do them."

I was a free-spirited teenager in the 1970s, and by the ninth grade I spent most of my extra time at work or with my high school boyfriend. I was one of the youngest and most petite girls in class, and to top it off, I struggled with being left-handed (in a right-handed world). School was a challenge for me also due to my dyslexia; I became quiet and withdrawn and didn't have much faith in myself. Thanks to my mom's reassurance, I managed to graduate as scheduled from Southwest High School in Fort Worth.

After high school, I was accepted to Miss Wade's Fashion Merchandising College, a trade school in Dallas, Texas, which is now known as Wade College. I earned an associate degree in fashion merchandising. After college, I chose to work for my dad as a cashier for the service and parts department of his car dealership. It wasn't until many years later in life that I would fulfill my dream to work in the fashion industry.

In my early twenties, my mom and I opened a wedding catering business. She was the "chief cook and bottle washer" (as she would say). I was the president and CEO, her sous chef, and the master wedding cake decorator. But my favorite part of the business was working with the brides to create their dream wedding. Mom and I sold the business after twelve years and great success.

Without realizing it growing up but looking back now, I learned a lot from my parents. Over time my father's influence in the business world helped me become a successful businesswoman. My mother's ability to nurture my strengths, despite my challenges, helped me grow into a strong, independent woman.

In 1997, I found the social selling industry to be my saving grace. This industry offered me flexibility, the ability to be my own boss, and income to contribute to the family budget. Because of my prior experience and success as a business owner, I quickly understood what it would take to be successful in this new venture.

To date I have worked in this industry for over twenty years, fourteen of them as an independent cabi stylist. Being a stylist has helped grow my leadership and coaching skills, which are essential in my newest adventure of supporting and coaching law enforcement officers wives with the challenges they face.

As I said earlier, my dream while growing up was to get married and have children, so you might be wondering how and when I met and married my husband. Let me take you back to 1975, after I'd graduated from trade school and was working at my dad's dealership.

One Friday in the summer, my high school friend Julie called me and insisted I spend the weekend with her. "Hey," she said, "we should go to Yesterday's Club! It's a cool bar close to where we grew up. You know, the kind of bar where everyone knows your name. I've been there a few times, and a lot of our high school friends meet up there on the weekends. Come on, it will be fun!"

I thought to myself, *I could use a night on the town.* I was nineteen years old, and the minimum drinking age back then was eighteen. "Sure, let's do it," I said. "I'll meet you there at 6:30."

Julie and I met in the parking lot and walked in together. The place was, well, virtually empty except for one macho-looking guy sitting in an elevated corner booth. He caught my eye because he reminded me of the Marlboro Man, a popular figure in television commercials for Marlboro cigarettes. He looked the part of the brand image—a masculine, rugged, confident cowboy with a cigarette in hand.

"Julie, you said everyone from high school hung out here," I commented disappointedly. "This place is almost empty!"

She laughed and said, "It's early, so chill. By 8 p.m. this place will be booming!" After a quick scan, she said, "Hey, I know that guy in the elevated corner booth! Let's go talk with him."

Puzzled, I looked at her and asked jokingly, "How do you know the Marlboro Man?"

"Oh, that's Jay," she said. She smiled, grabbed my arm and began dragging me, unwillingly, toward him. "He played football with my brother in high school," Julie said.

We walked up to the booth where Jay was sitting, and Julie introduced me. Our eyes met and lingered longer than usual. As I stumbled through a simple hello, I could feel my cheeks begin to blush. Jay immediately tipped his Stetson hat and smiled back at me. I later found out he thought to himself, *Wow, she's cute!*

"Have a seat, gals," he said nonchalantly. "I haven't seen y'all in here before. Is this your first time to Yesterday's Club?"

Talking over each other, Julie said, "No," and I said, "Yes."

Jay just laughed, and as we found our seats, he offered us a light for our cigarettes. Julie and I ordered a beer and some food to share.

As the evening progressed, I noticed my cheeks were sore from laughing and smiling. It had been a long time since I'd laughed so much. I thought to myself, *Now this guy is funny, or maybe it's just the beer.*

Yesterday's Club began to fill up with locals, and Julie went off to visit, but I only had eyes for Jay. It must have been mutual, because Jay never left his favorite elevated corner booth all evening. I'm not certain, but I bet if we had asked Julie later, she would have said, "You two both met your soul mate that night."

Jay and I discovered we had attended the same high school. It was no surprise we didn't know each other because he'd been a grade ahead of me and played sports. The only sports events I ever even attended in high school were the homecoming football games.

I also learned that Jay had totaled his Mach One a few weeks earlier and was without a car for a while. *What a bummer*, I thought to myself. *I guess he won't be asking me out on a date anytime soon.*

Hockey became the topic of conversation before the evening ended, and I told him, "I kinda like watching hockey!" Eventually he got up the nerve to ask for my phone number. After we'd exchanged numbers, I said bravely, "If you need a ride anywhere special, just give me a call."

Within a few days, Jay called. We continued our conversation about hockey. The time was right, so I asked, "Do you want to go to a hockey game on Friday? I can pick you up. My Toyota Celica ST, standard shift, will get us there."

"Sure," he said. "I'll pay for the tickets."

It was a date; so technically, I asked him out first!

Neither of us was "in hot pursuit" of love; however, it wasn't long before he began to chase me—or as he liked to say, "I chased her 'til she caught me."

Soon we began spending most of our spare time together. I enjoyed watching him play baseball and flag football. Football at that time was his passion. He would get so excited during football season he'd tell me, "I have little footballs running through my veins!"

Eventually we met each other's families. My dad helped Jay get a job working at a container manufacturing company where he made boxes and other types of containers. It was shift work that required brute strength. He would come over to my apartment a few times a week after work, exhausted from the physical labor.

As our relationship progressed, we began to share our life histories and our dreams with each other. I told him all I really wanted to be was a wife and mother—someday. He told me he was thinking about becoming a police officer—someday.

I began to fall in love with his humor, his big servant heart, and his protective nature. I also began to notice how passionate he was about what was important to him.

One day my father said, "Jay, I hear you like baseball. How would you like to take Vicki to a Texas Rangers baseball game sometime? My season tickets are on the front row, third base side!"

Jay's mouth dropped open, and his eyes grew big with excitement. "Yes sir! I'd love to take her to a major league baseball game!" Jay winked at me, and I thought, *Oh, now he has little baseballs running through his veins!* I looked at dad and said, "Who are the Texas Rangers?" He and Jay both laughed because they knew I was clueless.

Eighteen months later, after a few dozen Rangers games, drive-in movies, and late-night dinner dates, we became engaged.

I will never forget that evening. It was a very special night, November 11, 1976, and it was Jay's twenty-third birthday. I surprised him with his favorite meal of chicken and dumplings, and he surprised me with his proposal. We were married four months later, on February 5, 1977. I was twenty-one, and he was twenty-three years old. *My* dream was coming true.

Our standing joke we share with others, even to this day, is me saying, "The only reason Jay married me was for the front row seats at the Rangers games!" He laughs and says, "Well, it's not the *only* reason, but it's in the top three!"

Right before our wedding day, my dad offered Jay a job at his car dealership as a service advisor. Jay accepted. I continued to work as the cashier for the parts and service department. We drove to and from work together and had a very happy life, one I expected would continue for many years. What I didn't realize, however, was Jay had not forgotten about that dream he'd shared with me when we first met.

One evening, close to the end of our second year of marriage, Jay came home from work especially frustrated and restless. He shared with me that it was time for him to pursue *his* dream of becoming a police officer.

"This time," he said, "I want to get a job on my own! Not one that my parents or your dad give me. I want to do what I want to do."

I thought back to that time while we were dating when he shared his dream of becoming a police officer—someday. The day to pursue his dream actively had arrived. I, however, was skeptical, and I thought to myself, *This won't last long. I'm guessing he will play cops and robbers for a few years, get it out of his system, then go back to work for my dad—a secure and safe place to work.*

Forty-eight hours after our conversation, Jay applied to the Arlington Police Department. It was official. He was finally "in pursuit" of his own dream. On June 4, 1979, he began his 10-8 (in service) with the Arlington Police Department.

It was difficult for me to go into my dad's office and share the news about Jay applying to the police department. I was a bit nervous and unsure of what his response would be. He surprised me with these words of wisdom: "If you do something you love, you won't work a day in your life. If you do something you don't like, it becomes hard work."

I was glad he understood Jay's desire to become a police officer, but I'm not sure if I fully understood it at the time. It wasn't easy, at the age of twenty-three, to let go of the fantasy that my husband could possibly follow in my father's footsteps one day.

I'll never forget my dad's final words that day. "If Jay feels that's where he belongs, he should pursue it."

Debriefing

"Sometimes the smallest step in the right direction ends up being the biggest step in your life," I took my first step into my dream by asking Jay on a date. Jay took his first step to pursue his dream after we were married by applying to the APD to become a police officer.

Supporting each other's dreams, even if we don't understand them, is important. We don't know where they will take us, but we know the heart of our spouse. Both of us are grateful for the opportunity to live out our dreams with each other.

I encourage you to look back and reminisce on your first glance, first kiss and the moment when you became a "couple." Enjoy reminiscing on the past and the pleasure of pursuing one another and supporting each other's dreams.

Consider this Scripture verse as you respond to the bullet points that follow: Philippians. 2:3–4, "Do nothing out of selfish ambition or vain conceit. Rather, in humility value others above yourselves, not looking to your own interests but each of you to the interests of the others."

Bullet Points

Here are questions and thoughts for you to explore further.

- What circumstances brought the two of you together?
- Where can you see God's guiding hand in your decision to become a couple?
- What are your dreams? Why?
- How are you supporting your LEO's dreams?
- How is he supporting your dreams?

When I think of love this scripture comes to my mind: 1 Corinthians 13: 4–5, "Love is patient, love is kind. It does not envy, it does not boast, it is not proud. It does not dishonor others, it is not self-seeking, it is not easily angered, it keeps no record of wrongs."

BOLO 3

The Villain aka Worry and Fear

Be on the lookout for the villain (worry and fear) to hang out inside the minds of law enforcement officers wives. This unwelcomed intruder causes havoc, stress, and anxiety. Most women are nurturers by nature and tend to worry. We especially worry about our family, friends, and beloved pets. Our worries are usually short term. Unless a worry is about a life-threatening experience, we can, for the most part, manage to live with it. But when we see our spouses transform from happy-go-lucky guys to serious-minded law enforcement officers in uniform and hear what they experience, our worry and fear can increase to a dangerous level and become the villain we have to confront.

I N OCTOBER OF 1979, I found myself sitting on the edge of a seat in a police station briefing room, feeling somewhat out of place. The small, gray, dingy space began to fill up. Two tables to my left, draped with blue plastic tablecloths, were adorned with a punchbowl, coffee and donuts (of course), and a few trays of cookies. Up front I saw a makeshift podium with a row of chairs behind it for the panel of guest speakers and two bar stools off to the side. Folding chairs filled the rest of the room. From what I could tell based on the number of chairs; the department was expecting about twenty guests. I was glad to find a few seats in the middle for Jay and me so I wouldn't have to sit in the first or second row. But as a petite, five-foot-two-inch, one hundred-pounds-when-soaking-wet young woman, I wondered if I'd be able to see the speakers from there.

I squirmed but sat quietly, waiting impatiently for Jay to join me. I didn't know anyone there and wasn't quite sure about protocol for this nonmandatory, but highly recommended, meeting for police spouses. I had attended a few formal events during Jay's time at Basic Course in Applied Police Science (BCAPS) 48 Police Academy at the North Central Texas Regional Police Academy. However, none of the events were held at the police station. Even Jay's graduation ceremony, where I pinned badge #548 on his uniform just a few weeks prior, was held in a large auditorium. So entering the police station for the first time was pretty intimidating, especially for this young, naïve twenty-three-year-old.

Jay entered the room and found his seat next to mine. I did a double take. Seeing him dressed as a police officer was still so fresh to me. He looked so official and authoritative, and I was impressed. Pride beamed through his eyes. I smiled nervously and then felt his firm hand pat me on the leg, as always, to assure me all would be okay.

I sat up straight, feeling awkward. *I'd better behave,* I thought to myself. *Deep breath, Vicki. Just breathe!*

High-ranking police supervisors of the City of Arlington Texas Police Department entered the room and filled the seats up front. The room quieted. The chaplain of the police department, Harold Elliott, opened the meeting with a prayer. Next, the then Chief of Police Herman C. Perry made his way to the podium. He welcomed everyone and turned the microphone over to the first speaker on the panel.

One by one, sergeants, lieutenants, and deputy chiefs spoke about what was to come and what our husbands would conceivably experience because of the role they now had in society, especially in our community.

I don't remember what my expectations were before that meeting, but I listened to every word and took mental notes on how my husband was going to change and what my unwritten responsibility was about to become. Slowly, what I'd unknowingly signed up for just two and a half years earlier on February 5, 1977, when I autographed my marriage certificate became real. I was a police officer's wife now, but I had no clue what that really meant.

When they were finished, the panel of speakers cleared the room. Next on the agenda to speak were an officer and his wife. He was dressed in plain clothes, and she seemed pleasant and welcoming. Suddenly the atmosphere in the room felt casual. I could feel myself begin to relax.

This couple pulled up the two barstools, which I'd noticed at the side, to sit on and casually shared their fifteen-year experience and expertise about marriage in the police profession. As upbeat and positive as they could be, they unfolded what their life was like. They shared statistics revealing that the divorce rate in law enforcement marriages is extremely high, around 75 percent, which is 25 percent higher than outside the profession.

The husband spoke of how police officers might, over time, isolate themselves from society. The wife shared how she kept him connected to family and friends by joining organizations, such as a church, bowling league or a golf club which offered opportunities for them to do things together with people who weren't associated with the law enforcement community. She expressed how her husband had a hard time relaxing when he was home. Even the little things in life seemed serious to him.

Wow, that's sad, I thought to myself. *I can't imagine Jay taking life so seriously. He has such a lighthearted personality and a great sense of humor.*

Together they talked about how to keep the communication lines open and how important communication would become over time. He shared how officers tend to bottle up what their day was really like so they won't worry their loved ones. She shared how she kept their communication open—she would let him know what was TMI (too much information) or NEI (not enough information). Both could quickly turn into worry and fear. I had a feeling it wouldn't take me long to experience what she meant.

Before Jay became a cop, I didn't put much thought into how I handled worry and fear. But that night we both heard loudly and clearly these would become reoccurring emotions for me. I had never considered that Jay might conceal what his day was actually like so I wouldn't worry. Now I was worrying about the possibility of worrying!

I felt my chest tighten as my personal, imaginary bulletproof vest began to mold itself around my upper body like a shield of steel. From that point on, this vest became part of my daily outfit. I would wear it to protect my heart and provide me with the strength, courage, and confidence I didn't even know existed inside me.

I had little experience or concern with worry or fear in my life up to that point, but on that evening I began to wonder how I would deal with the issues that lurked ahead of us. After arriving home and realizing my need for help in this area, I thought to myself, *If I am going to get ahead of this villain, then I need to understand it.*

I looked up the words *worry* and *fear* in the dictionary, and here's what I found:

> **Worry**—give way to anxiety or unease, allow one's mind to dwell on difficulty or troubles; a state of anxiety and uncertainty over actual or potential problems.

> **Fear**—a distressing emotion aroused by impending danger, evil, pain, etc., whether the threat is real or imagined; the feeling or condition of being afraid.

A few words stood out to me: "actual or potential" and "real or imagined."

I stayed awake that evening, waiting for Jay to return from completing his shift with his training officer. Once he was home, we talked about what we'd learned from the meeting. We discussed his willingness to stay connected with people outside the world of law enforcement. We talked in depth about how my possible worries and fears could escalate. We agreed to keep the lines of communication open. When we found ourselves struggling between TMI and NEI, we agreed that he would do his best to help me through whatever struggles I was having. Most importantly, we talked about how important our marriage vows were to each other. We agreed to do whatever it took to be in the twenty-fifth percentile of law enforcement marriage statistics.

As time passed, I learned there were a lot of so-called, "routine days." Days when Jay went to work came home on time, and transitioned into his role of husband and eventually father with ease. But, as expected and in reality, there was no such thing as a routine call at work for him to respond to. And I also learned firsthand what it felt like to experience the villain, that unwelcomed intruder.

The real-life stories Jay shared with me along with the daily reminders of how vulnerable police officers can be are blasted on the television, in newspapers, and in current time social media, made me realize how important my imaginary bulletproof vest was.

By the end of Jay's rookie year, I found myself pacing the floors during the times he came home late, worrying over actual or potential dangers he was facing. My personal time clock would tell me when his shift was over and when he should walk in the door. When there was no sign of him, my mind would begin to battle with the villain.

What was keeping him? What "routine" call was he working on? Would I see him on the news? Should I turn on the news?

When he didn't arrive home on time and his delay grew longer with no word or sign of him coming up the driveway, an uncomfortable knot in my gut would begin to tighten. I would rehearse over and over in my mind how I would handle the situation if Chaplain Elliott and a close fellow officer appeared at my door instead of him. Sadly, I had rehearsed it so often it was like an old movie, a classic—one in which I knew the characters, the lives, the pain, and the sadness in their faces. In this scene at my door, no words were ever spoken. Just the presence of them at the door would say it all.

I'd tell myself during the long wait, *if the doorbell actually rings, I just wouldn't answer it. Then it wouldn't be real.*

I wondered if I'd ever get over the constant battle between my head and my heart. Did I have the strength inside me to do this, not just one night, but over and over again?

In the early years of Jay's career, phone communication wasn't as easy as it is today. Those brief mobile phone communications, which are life-giving for today's LEOWs, seldom happened back then. Instead, Jay would have to stop at a pay phone to call me, so you can imagine how often that happened! His reasons, *aka* excuses for not calling when he was working late, were either weather related, he didn't have a quarter with him, or my favorite—he didn't want to wake me. As if I was asleep anyway.

My timeline for worry would begin when I realized he wasn't at home on time. Sometimes his arrival home would be hours later, without any communication. When my worries surfaced the villain showed up in my mind, armed and ready for battle and when this emotion of worry would evolve into fear, the villain would show signs of winning the battle. In contrast, today's police wives may begin to worry within minutes because he hasn't texted back, and fear quickly follows.

I began to recognize I needed strength, courage, understanding, and also faith in God and a lot of time in prayer to keep the villain from creeping into my mind. I had so much to learn, especially how to rely on faith and prayer.

Jay and I joined a church and became active in a small group that met on Tuesday evenings, which was his day off. As my faith and understanding grew over time, I began to rely on God for peace and comfort. Over time, the "armor of God" the Bible talks about and my imaginary bulletproof vest became sufficient.

Debriefing

Some days may be hard, but you can do this! You can fight the villain and win the battle too. Although my timeline for the villain of worry and fear to surface may seem different than your experience, because of the ability to communicate with a simple text, but the feelings are the same.

Your experience of battling the villain may escalate quickly and appear more like JoAnne's recently occurrence. She told me,

> After my boys were in bed I texted Robert. He didn't respond. I waited a few minutes and texted him again, no response. I began to worry. I knew worrying wasn't good for me and couldn't change anything, but I felt it coming on. I tried to stay busy, but my mind wouldn't stop so I decided to text him on last time. No response. I got online to check the patrol log for his district and see what calls were happening in his beat. There was a domestic call happening in his beat, which are the worst. So now my worry escalated into fear. I could feel my heart rate rising as I imagined the worst. When he finally contacted me, I was relieved to say the least. He wasn't even on that domestic call, his phone was on silent and he was safe. It just happens so fast sometimes. Going from thinking that he's safe to thinking the worst.

JoAnne's example of how worry and fear can escalate happens more often than we'd like to admit. Fear of the worst-case scenario can bring this villain to surface. I'm rather envious of the LEOWs who have the villain totally under control, especially early in their husband's career. Marcie, whose husband works for Fort Worth PD on patrol, said she doesn't worry about him. Sarah, whose husband is with the Irving PD and has been undercover for over eight years, also told me that she doesn't worry about her husband either. She said, "None of us know when our time here on earth is finished. I have faith and confidence in my husband. He knows what he's doing and takes the proper precautions to stay safe."

I discovered that the Bible says we are not supposed to worry. It's an emotion we are supposed to give to God. Let go and let God. Let him fight the villain.

Bullet Points

What can you do to cope with the villain, *worry and fear*? Consider these bullet points.

- Understand that worry and fear are common emotions.
- Sometimes these emotions are justified.
- Learn what triggers your worry and fear so you can start to control them.
- Recognize when you worry too often.
- Give yourself permission to limit your time on social media and the news, which could trigger your emotions and keep the villain working overtime.
- Anxiety can be crippling. Just breathe!
- Find techniques to calm your anxious heart.
- Refocus your thoughts on what is right and good.
- There are apps you can download on your phone that offer relaxation and meditation.
- Keep the lines of communication open. His TMI and NEI can be a constant, challenging issue.
- Trust in your LEO's ability to do his job well. The powerful strength of Jay's self-assurance was a comfort to me.
- Find support through family, friends, and the police community.
- Become active in a church and develop friends of faith who will pray for you and your husband.
- Turn to God in prayer and lean on him.

Philippians 4: 6–7 says, "Do not be anxious about anything, but in every situation, by prayer and petition, with thanksgiving present your requests to God. And the peace of God, which transcends all understanding, will guard your hearts and your minds in Christ Jesus."

BOLO 4

Answering the Call

Be on the lookout for your husband to answer God's call
to become a law enforcement officer. In the beginning,
he may not realize the depth of God's will for him to
protect and serve. As time goes on, he may need to find
balance and peace in being a Christian and an officer.
Answering the call to become a police officer involves
intense training and commitment to department values
and standards. And because he wears the badge, you are
on the journey with him. You too have a calling to answer.

WHEN JAY BECAME A police officer, at first we didn't grasp
the concept of God's call for him, much less my calling
in this journey as a LEO wife. We simply were going
through the motions of our lives, without the understanding of what
it meant to be "called by God" for a purpose greater than ourselves.
However, after a few years of living in the world of law enforcement,

we began to see the correlation between the job, God's calling for him, and how important it was for Jay to have my support and understanding.

Patrol officers spend most of their shift answering calls, responding to a wide variety of situations. Some are minor, and some are major in nature. In one day, calls can range from responding to a felony, handling a misdemeanor, and investigating a 9–1–1 hang up. When officers respond to these calls, they are called to do so with integrity, honor, and a servant heart. Why? Because doing so is more than a job. In my opinion, they do so because they are called by God to protect and serve.

For Detective Allan Hudson, serving on the police force is a lifelong calling. "Most people working in the public service sector feel their job is something they were made to do," he said. "I was made to be a police officer." Serving the public is at the center of Detective Hudson's life, as evidenced by his work as a LEO and service in the Texas Air National Guard.

"Our souls are not hungry for fame, comfort, wealth or power," says Rabbi Harold Kushner. "Our souls are hungry for meaning, for the sense that we have figured out how to live so that our lives matter, so that the world will be at least a little bit different for our having passed through it."

The Arlington Police Department's vision statement is "Service before self, honor above all." You may ask, what does that mean? I would say it means they are called to have a servant heart toward others and demonstrate it by being servants of the community and God. They put others first, even to the point of sacrificing their own lives to save others.

Serving with honor, as I understand it, means being an honest and noble person. Keeping your word and being fair. Jay says it best in fewer words. "Police work is an honorable job."

I have noticed that Jay's heart of serving others with honor first is part of his God-given nature. At our church, he volunteers to usher, assuring everyone has a seat. During communion time, Jay and the other ushers are the last group to take communion, making sure all others have been served first. These examples are not job related. They are part of who Jay is, living out his calling. Although he doesn't recognize the correlation, I see it clearly.

The Arlington Police Department's core values, as stated on their website, are integrity, compassion and fairness. Jay has always told me, "Integrity is doing the right thing even when nobody is watching." To help you understand what each of these values means in the life of an officer, I share here a few examples.

Many years ago, the APD created police trading cards for several officers. Jay handed out his trading cards to children of all ages. His card had a picture of him on the front and a quote from him on the back. His quote said, "Use your God-given skills, talents, and senses. If something looks wrong or feels wrong, it's probably wrong. Remember to strive to do the right thing, at the right time, the right way, for the right reason." These cards became his way to encourage others he met to exhibit integrity in their lives.

Compassion, another of the department's core values, has been evident in my husband's humble ways. As an example, about every three months for over thirty years, he has donated his blood to our local blood bank. It is a selfless, putting-others-first act of compassion. Little did we know as he did so over the years just how important this act of compassion would become for us personally. A few years ago, our daughter had to have four blood transfusions to help save her life after the difficult delivery of her first child. She became a recipient of someone's generous, life-giving blood donation.

The core value of fairness is a daily act in an officer's life. Whether it's a domestic dispute, a car accident, or whatever incidents they encounter.

It is, as Jay says, "There are usually at least two sides to the story. And we listen to all sides of each situation as to determine how best to handle the incident. Officers gather all the information from the suspect, the victim, and witnesses. Officers then, in all fairness, enforce the law and protect the innocent. We write a report and, if necessary, make an arrest and take violators to jail. We are not the judge and jury."

As I said earlier, police officers fulfill, knowingly or unknowingly, what God has called them to do for others. Chaplain Harold Elliott once said, "Police officers, in a sense, *minister* to others. They don't even realize that is what they are doing." Here is one example.

Chaplain Elliott and an officer were called out to a death investigation. A young mother, living in very poor conditions, had just lost her infant child. Through her tears she said, "I need to leave for work." The chaplain and the officer encouraged her to stay home and grieve over the loss of her baby, but she told them she couldn't. She would not be able to pay for the next few days' rent and would be back out on the street.

"It was a sad situation," Chaplain Elliott said. "The officer knew he couldn't just hand this young woman money for rent, so he privately donated the money to my ministry and asked if I would offer it to her."

From that day on, from time to time, this officer would make a donation to Chaplain Elliott's ministry and say to him, "When you cross paths with someone in desperate need, please offer this money to them." Even after the officer retired from the police department, the chaplain would receive an envelope filled with money to continue with his ministry. This officer demonstrated a genuine example of a servant heart and compassion for others.

Chaplain Elliott also shared with me about a very difficult time in his family's life, a time when his family experienced the tragic loss of their daughter, Tina Sue. Her death was ruled "undetermined."

"Within minutes of hearing of our loss," he said, "our home began to fill with officers. They knew just what to do. They immediately took control and ministered to us. These officers filled our refrigerator and pantry with food, drinks, and paper goods. I remember vividly seeing one police officer come in with a large bag of toilet paper. These officers thought of our most basic needs. They knew we would have family and friends coming and going in the days ahead, and they provided everything we needed."

Police officers, or as many like to say, "peace officers," dedicate their lives to serving others and helping their communities be a better place to live. Most are educated, intelligent, strong, loyal, courageous, and dedicated individuals. The clear majority are a far cry from what Hollywood portrays them to be, which is mostly uneducated, lazy, guns-blazing, overweight, coffee drinkers and donut eaters, and sometimes corrupt.

I began to wonder about the origin of Hollywood's depiction and discovered some interesting background. It is my presumption that the "coffee and donuts" myth began developing in the late 1940s. At that time, the only places to eat at four in the morning were all-night diners serving coffee and donuts. Without any other options, weary midnight shift cops would stop in for caffeine and a snack. When motion pictures began capturing the image, cops would forever be immortalized as coffee drinkers and donut dunkers. I wish our husband's job was as easy as stopping in a diner for a simple, early morning breakfast!

Interestingly, many officers today are "health nuts" and wouldn't eat a donut unless they knew their CrossFit class was next on their schedule. It should not be a surprise that the majority of today's LEOs are healthy and fit. Answering the call to become a police officer involves physical, intense training as well as commitment to department values and standards.

For police officers to do their duty well, they begin their career at the training division. Training at a police academy is long and demanding, physically and emotionally. It also takes away from their family time. When they are at home, much of their time is spent studying for the next exam and working on their skills. As an example, Jay had to be physically fit, master hand-to-hand combat, qualify on the firing range with a handgun and shotgun, learn handcuffing techniques, and master emergency and pursuit driving skills. He had to learn the use of an ASP (expandable baton), OC spray (pepper), and Taser. In addition, he had to literally memorize the "use of force continuum", which means—their presence in uniform, their words (speech), physical force, non-lethal force and deadly force.

The training doesn't stop at physical skills. It includes verbal communication, *aka* "verbal judo" and learning how to work within the extensive rules and procedures of the law and the community. Officers also must become knowledgeable about their local and state laws and the U.S. Constitution. Several constitutional amendments are relevant to police officers.

When Jay was at home during training, it was my job to help him master his 10 codes (a form of communication) and signal codes (radio traffic, instead of plain language), both are quick ways to communicate. He also had to learn all the city ordinances, penal codes, and traffic laws. Partnering with him as he learned gave me a glimpse of what his career was going to be like.

Officer Robert recently went through the APD Academy, so I asked him about the current qualifications and training process. The conversation reminded me that the APD, like other departments around the country, has very high standards for becoming an officer. A bachelor's degree is required to apply. Robert had a master's degree at the time he applied. Other departments may require at least an associate degree.

Robert worked briefly for another police department before he applied to Arlington. During the basic training academies for it and APD, he earned the highest recognition for his physical fitness scores. He was elected Class President by his peers at one department, nominated for the APD Rookie of the Year, and most recently completed a two-week Basic SWAT training course.

JoAnne, Robert's wife, told me that both academies he attended were very long and demanding, physically and emotionally. She said,

> When Robert was going through the APD's academy, I was pregnant with our second child. I was grateful and lucky Robert could be there for the delivery, but of course he couldn't take any extra time off after the birth of our son. I had to rely on family to help us through the first few weeks. Sadly, a month after our son was born, I had a health issue that required a brief hospital stay for an emergency procedure. Robert could not be there by my side. It was difficult. But we

made it through. Looking back, I believe it helped me recognize the responsibility of his job and the sacrifices I would have to endure.

The APD's mission statement says, "The Arlington Police Department will build trust in the community through transparent actions and positive engagement and will leverage technology, geographic policing, and employee development to increase legitimacy and reduce crime." For Jay, this mission translated to him as an example; conducting meetings and helping develop neighborhood crime watch programs throughout the city.

Before beginning their duties, police officers take and subscribe to an oath. Every two years they reaffirm this oath. In their oath, the officers swear to uphold the U.S. Constitution and the laws within their jurisdiction. Police officers further swear to complete the duties of their position and behave honorably and with good conduct to the best of their abilities. The oath of affirmation is filed in the office of the city secretary.

As LEOWs, you and I are called to something greater than ourselves too, and it includes supporting our husband in his calling. Striving for that balance and peace in *our* calling leads us to find the courage and strength to make it through the tough times: the "lost" times when we struggle to dig deep inside for the right support to offer him, and the scary times when we fear for our husband's safety.

Though LEOWs' "oath of affirmation" is not filed anywhere, ours too is truly a noble calling, one for each of us to recognize and revere as we help our officers fulfill their call.

Debriefing

Officers begin their career with the best of intentions and a compelling calling. "However," Jay says, "the job changes us. We learn quickly that we didn't write the laws but we are duty bound to enforce them. To keep the peace, we have to stop the disturbance. The idea of helping people turns into dealing with drunks, people who are mentally ill, thieves, robbers, abusers, and murderers. We rescue the victims, but more than likely we also have to arrest someone else."

When officers have encounters with people who inflict cruelty on others, these encounters change them. For some officers, their attitudes about the nature of what they must do may have an adverse effect on them over time. They become cynical, have trust issues, and become suspicious of everyone. This mindset can harden their hearts and cause them to lose sight of their calling.

I have seen glimpses of this sad aspect of the job in my husband and later in Robert, who is only a few years into his career. Other officers and police wives have shared the same observation with me. Maybe all officers must go through some transformation so they can do their job and do it well, day after day and year after year. However, when we see it happen to our officers, it is good to remember the words of Ephesians 4:1, "I urge you to live a life worthy of the calling you have received."

Many Christian LEO families hold dear certain Scripture passages. A very popular Scripture verse for police officers is Matthew 5:9, "Blessed are the peacemakers, for they will be called children of God." This verse reminds them of their part of the job that is keeping the peace.

The patron saint of police officers is Saint Michael the Archangel. He represents the values of bravery, courage, and justice. A few years ago, I found a hand-carved, wooden statue of Saint Michael and put it on display in our home. It is a reminder that God is with Jay, wherever he goes. What do you have to remind you of the same for your husband?

Police departments do not permit officers to display their faith on their uniform, so Jay carried a cross in his pocket and a prayer in his wallet. He also had his father's pocket version of the New Testament Bible in his briefcase. These resources kept him grounded in the what and why of his job, his calling.

I encourage you to spend time with the questions that follow. If you are a Christian, you can pray for God's wisdom and understanding. After you have answered them, discuss them with your husband. This Scripture verse might help.

"We have different gifts, according to the grace given to each of us. If your gift is prophesying, then prophesy in accordance with your faith; if it is serving, then serve; if it is teaching, then teach; if it is to encourage, then give encouragement; if it is giving, then give generously; if it is to lead, do it diligently; if it is to show mercy, do it cheerfully." Romans 12:6–8

1. Do you feel your husband is called by God to do the work of God?
2. How has this chapter changed your thinking about your husband's answer to God's calling?
3. Does your husband struggle with the idea that the work he does is God's work? If so, how can you remind him of the good work he is doing?
4. How do you see integrity, compassion, fairness, honesty, and service in your husband's everyday life?
5. How do you feel about the idea that God has placed you in your husband's life to support him in his calling?
6. Do you feel that you too are called to something greater than yourself? If so, what?
7. What can you do to lessen the burden and accept the idea that he is called to be a peace officer?
8. How does this chapter help you worry less about him, knowing that God is with him wherever he goes?

Bullet Points

Here are ideas and thoughts for you to explore further.

- If you ever get to Clare City, Michigan, try to visit the popular diner named Cops and Donuts—Clare City Bakery. I have not been there, but it is part of a popular chain. There is another one named Cops and Donuts, Jay's Precinct, in Gaylord, Michigan. The website (https://copsdoughnuts.com/) says, "Real Cops, Real Donuts!" and gives the following as their mission: "Dedicated to inspiring and develop great people who will delight our guests and improve the cops and donuts portfolio for the benefit of all."

- You might consider joining an organization that offers Christian support. Fellowship of Christian Peace Officers—USA ((http://www.fcpo.org/) is one that has been around for a long time.

- Shield a Badge with a Prayer is a ministry that was started in our area by one of Jay's coworkers, Tim Henz, and his family members (www.shield-a-badge.org/). Tim says, "Our organization is free, and we will be happy to help you start this ministry in your area."

- Look for classes and books. At one time my church offered a Bible study for law enforcement officers called "The Peacekeepers" based on a book by Michael Dye. A good book is *Honor Begins at Home* by Michael Catt and Steven and Alex Kendrick.

- Consider starting a small group for LEOWs or a Bible study in your area. I currently offer a weekly Bible study specifically for wives of law enforcement officers. We have found it to be a comfort zone to open up and be in community with others who understand the unique struggles and challenges we face.

Romans 8:28 says, "And we know that in all things God works for the good of those who love him, who have been called according to his purpose."

BOLO 5

Guard Your Heart

Be on the lookout for hurtful slings and arrows in the form of words that may come your way. Guard your heart from the pain of being excluded, rejected and isolated because your spouse is in law enforcement.

I REMEMBER VIVIDLY, IN THE beginning of Jay's career, the feeling of a close friend becoming unexpectedly distant. Our relationship became strained, awkward, and off balance from what it had been. I wish I could say this experience was just a natural progression of friends growing apart in their early twenties. There was, however, an underlying reason to this particular relationship separation: exclusion.

Angela and I were close friends, so it wasn't unusual for us to talk a few times each week. We'd grown up on the same street, gone to the same schools, and taken gymnastics together. She was even a bridesmaid in my wedding. My simple "hello, how's it's going" check-in with her that day was common and innocent enough. But the conversation we had caught me off guard.

It was mid-April 1980 around 7:30 in the evening. I was twenty-four years old and six-months pregnant with our first child. Jay was a rookie cop. That day happened to be the first week of his 13-week rotation on the evening shift. We were both in the process of getting adjusted to his new schedule.

I finished my "solo" evening meal and then placed the dish in the sink. Before walking back to the table, I picked up the phone, which was plugged into the wall, and then dialed Angela's number. As I walked back to the table, the long, extended, rubber-coiled cord of the times followed. My kitchen table was nestled in the nook of the bay window, and the blinds were open to view the beauty of springtime. I silently wondered if any of the friendly hummingbird visitors were fluttering right outside the windows. Jay and I had strategically secured a feeder for them on a branch of our beautiful dwarf magnolia tree.

Right before I sat down, my eyes danced a quick glance toward the feeder in hopes of seeing one or two, but no such luck. Then my eyes moved toward the floor, and I could clearly see it was time to prop up my feet to keep the new experience of swelling to a minimum. About the time Angela answered, up went my feet.

Our conversation, as usual, began with small talk, but unexpectedly Angela slipped in a comment about a recent weekend party Jay and I apparently had not been invited to. In my surprised "I can't believe this, BFF (best friend forever)" tone, I asked for more details. Angela hesitated and then began to stumble over her words. I could feel myself getting tense. Unconsciously I began to swirl the phone cord around my finger, over and over. My finger began to throb from this mindless activity, but at the moment I was more interested in asking her questions than releasing the pain from my finger.

I pressed her. "Why don't you tell me what's *really* going on?"

Angela had delayed shooting the arrow to my heart as long as she could. Reluctantly she said, "Y'all were not invited because Jay's a police officer now. Think about it, Vicki. Who wants a cop to show up at their party?"

Ouch, that hurt.

After her disclosure, we had little more to say to each other, so our conversation ended. I stared out the window in silence and let her remarks of being excluded soak in. Repeating her words over and over in my mind, I let the tears begin to flow.

I was able to stop the throbbing sensation in my finger by unwrapping the phone cord that was constricting the blood flow, but it didn't help to ease the anxious, throbbing feeling in my heart.

At times like this one, the urge to call my BFF and cry on her shoulder normally would have been strong. Well, Angela was my best friend.

I felt alone and rejected.

Jay arrived home from his shift around 11:30 and recognized I was upset. He immediately sat down beside me on the sofa, patted me on the leg, and asked, "What's the matter, dear? Why have you been crying?"

I told him about the conversation with Angela and repeated her painful comment: "Think about it, Vicki. Who wants a cop to show up at their party?"

Tears began to flow again. "We weren't invited," I sobbed, "because you're a police officer now."

Jay looked at me with compassion, shook his head, and said, "I'm sorry, dear." Kissing me and then reaching out to hold my hands in his, he then said bluntly those four words that are so telling: "Get used to it."

Jay continued, trying to put our new lifestyle into perspective and help me face a new reality. "We will be excluded from some parties and events from now on, dear. My profession requires people to look at me differently. I know you see me as Jay, but some will only see a police officer. Even when we are invited in the future to these events, my shift schedule may limit us from going anyway."

I took a good look at the man holding my hands and consoling me. He was compassionate and understanding. Oh, by the way, he was still wearing his police uniform. There was something powerful in that uniform I couldn't deny.

Jay was right. This man, or I should say *policeman*, with his "command presence and authority to arrest," was not going to be invited to certain social gatherings too often; therefore, neither would I.

I thought to myself, *Jay said to "get used to it." But how does someone get used to being excluded and feeling rejected?* I felt the urge to sit up straight and take a few extra deep breaths, one for me and one for the child I was carrying. As I did, I could sense the strength of my imaginary bulletproof vest wrapped around me. I used it this time to protect my heart—from slings and arrows, especially the ones from close friends.

With renewed strength in my voice, I said to Jay, "I'll be fine. It was just a dumb party anyway."

Jay smiled and lightened the air with one of his corny one-liners. "I guess she didn't want her party to be a *bust*, huh?"

I chuckled. "Cute, Jay."

You may be wondering what happened with Angela and our friendship. Well, the conversation we had was an indication that our lifestyles were going in different directions. We had a long history together, so the change was gradual. We grew apart, as many childhood friendships do. However, from time to time, we would touch base with a "hello, how's it going" check in with each other.

Debriefing

So, my LEOW sisters, how can you manage the sadness of feeling excluded and rejected or even losing a friend because you are married to a law enforcement officer? Exclusion and rejection can sometimes turn into fear, especially if you are caught off guard. Fear can surface in many forms, but the one that stands out the most is the fear you will not measure up to someone else's view of what is believed to be true. You may find yourself in a state of isolation, feeling lonely and alone.

My best advice is to try not to let yourself worry about what others think, or allow the hurtful comments of others send you into isolation. I certainly don't have all the answers, but here are a few tips from my personal experience.

Bullet Points

Here are ideas and thoughts for you to explore further.

- Be proud of who you are.
- Some people may instantly judge you in a negative way simply because you are married to a LEO. The judgment can be difficult. You may be taken aback. But guard your heart with your imaginary bulletproof vest and this promise from Scripture: "The peace of God, which transcends all understanding, will guard your hearts and your minds in Christ Jesus" (Philippians 4:7).
- It's okay to let go of a few relationships that no longer fit in the law enforcement lifestyle. Doing so might be painful at first, but it will be better in the long run for everyone involved. When you feel a relationship is becoming strained and unbalanced because your husband is a LEO, pray about the relationship. Ask God for guidance, and accept the results. Use this promise as comfort: "Trust in the LORD with all your heart and lean not on your own understanding; in all your ways submit to him, and he will make your paths straight" (Proverbs 3:5–6).
- Make a conscious effort to avoid isolation. Find new girlfriends inside our Blue Nation and outside the world of law enforcement that are a better fit. Over time your social calendar will be full again.

- When meeting new people and exchanging information about spouse's careers, be prepared by being armored with your imaginary bulletproof vest and ready for their response. Silently rejoice and be pleasantly happy with positive responses.
- When people's body language or verbal comments show their negative mindset about police officers, try not to take it personally. Make a mental note to approach potential friendships with caution or not at all based on their responses to you. Here is an example, which has happened to me more than once: "Wow, you are married to a police officer? That surprises me. How could you stay married to him?" When comments like these arise, take heart and know this person clearly has a narrow mindset; therefore, developing a relationship more than likely would not be wise.
- Don't let feeling excluded, rejected or isolated define you. Understand that the people who reject you or your husband because of his career are the ones that have the issues, not you.
- Count your blessings, not your friends.
- Many cops don't want to be put in a situation that could jeopardize their badge or take legal action against a friend or relative. It's okay to decline a few invitations that could be questionable.
- Throw your own parties. You can control the guest list and the activities. You have the best to offer anyway, because as it's been said, "It's not a great party till the cops show up!"

Let these words of Scripture from Isaiah 41:9 encourage you: "I called you. I said, 'You are my servant'; I have chosen you and have not rejected you."

BOLO 6

Family Disturbances

Be on the lookout for "outlaws" who live among us. I'm sure you will agree, we all love our family, even in the tough times. You may have someone close to you whose lifestyle is not on the right side of the law. You may find yourself in the middle of a head-on collision between the "cops and robbers." The challenge is balancing relationships and setting up healthy boundaries.

YOUR HUSBAND, THE POLICE officer, will be dispatched to many family disturbance calls during his career on patrol. If you are a law enforcement family with both officers and outlaws in your family, know you are not alone. When a family disturbance hits close to home, it can be difficult to handle for everyone, especially you and your LEO.

An outlaw can be an immediate family member or a distant relative, a second cousin, an aunt or uncle. Maybe this outlaw is technically outside the "family tree," such as a BFF or another long-term relationship. Whatever situation you face, healthy boundaries and balance are important steps to coexisting.

Beverly, a police officer's wife who experienced a "cops and robbers" family disturbance, shared her story. Beverly's younger sister, Allison, was involved in an armed robbery along with her boyfriend. The police were dispatched immediately to the scene. Before Allison and her boyfriend knew it, they were in a shoot-out with the cops. The boyfriend was killed. By the grace of God, Allison walked away without injury.

During the beginning of my interview with Beverly, she told me, "The car ultimately looked like Bonnie and Clyde's last stand. What was most difficult for me and my husband to watch was my family rallying around Allison as if she were a victim instead of a willing participant in the robbery."

Allison was eventually convicted and sent to prison. About six months into her sentence, Beverly's parents convinced her to go with them to visit her sister.

"Vicki, as you can imagine, my husband was against the idea," Beverly said with a sigh. "I felt stuck in the middle, between my parents and my husband, the cop. I love my parents and Allison. I didn't want to disappoint them anymore because they had been through so much already. Neither did I want to go against my husband's wishes. Everyone wanted to find peace with the situation."

What a difficult position to be in, I thought to myself. Her family members were tugging at her heartstrings to have compassion for her sister, and her husband was telling her to stay away and not get too close.

Ultimately Beverly decided to go with her parents to visit with her sister.

I asked her, "What was it like to visit your sister in prison?" She sighed deeply then replied, "I felt so uncomfortable. Then wondered if I should have listened to my husband's wishes. On entering the prison walls, my parents and I were required to pass through many security checkpoints before reaching the prisoner visitation room. At each checkpoint, guards would open the thick, heavy metal, eerie looking doors, each with lights and alarms. As we were guided past each one, it would instantly slam shut behind us with a loud, clanging sound. The last one brought chills down my back. Suddenly I felt claustrophobic and trapped. I just wanted to escape, run back home to my husband, and feel safe and secure."

Beverly then shared what it was like after her sister completed her sentence. "Allison was released from prison. It wasn't long before she went back to the world of drugs, petty crime, and eventually prostitution. Her lifestyle led her into a vicious cycle of street life traumas, jail cells, rehabilitation facilities, and sobriety."

Beverly told me, "On one occasion my parents asked me to find out if my husband could assist them in rescuing Allison from a seedy location." This request was a clear lack of understanding and knowledge on their part of the oath police officers live by. Instinctively Beverly came to her husband's defense, telling her parents that without a doubt he could not assist them. "I'm not sure they appreciated my answer," she said, "but at the very least, it helped us begin to set boundaries."

I know with certainty how difficult it is to deal with a police officer, an outlaw, and family viewpoints. Like Beverly and her husband, we had our own family disturbance and had to balance these issues as they arose.

During Jay's training, his paperwork had been "red flagged" and eventually made it all the way to the top of the department. Jay was summoned to Chief Perry's office to answer some questions before he could proceed further in his training.

I believe Jay was nervous. Who wouldn't be? After all, the Chief did not personally interview most candidates. To this day, the memory of that meeting remains vivid in Jay's memory. "I'll never forget it," he said. "I was only twenty-five at the time, and the meeting had a lasting effect on me."

As I was writing this chapter, Jay sat down at our kitchen table and recollected the meeting as if it were yesterday. Jay recalled,

Right before entering the Chief's office, I gathered my composure. I wasn't really sure what this meeting was about. Closing the door behind me, almost instantly and in a deep voice of authority, Chief Perry said, 'Jay, have a seat.' I remember sitting down in the chair, which was directly across from him. I recall wanting to feel confident as to not show how nervous I was. Then, eye to eye with each other, Chief Perry said, 'Son, tell me about your association with this outlaw. You know, Jay, as an officer of the law, you are not to have any association with a convicted felon.' I paused, then answering truthfully, 'Yes sir, I understand. I absolutely do not have a close association with this person.' After the meeting was over, which was quick by the way, I took the summons to heart because the Chief was watching me. I needed to keep my distance from this particular individual, or it could cost me my career.

Jay told me later, "Looking back, I'm sure the Chief had to document our conversation."

Fortunately, Jay managed to satisfy the Chief and was able to move forward with his training. Ironically, while his badge was brand new, still shiny and bright like his future with the APD, the reality check of the "cops and robbers" family disturbance scenario felt closer than ever. When Jay was assigned to his FTO (field training officer), he discovered his FTO was one of the officers involved in that felony offense and had fired shots at and assisted in the arrest of the outlaw in the situation.

Just like Beverly and her LEO, we had to deal with setting boundaries and balancing family disturbance relationships. It was difficult and the emotional pull was tiring. Many feelings, including our own, were hurt. Emotions ran high. I personally didn't handle certain situations well and learned the hard way that you can't please all sides. At times the law enforcement perspective (just the facts) carried less weight than faith, hope, and love. Faith was always stronger than reality, hope was deeper than truth, and love forgave every time.

I eventually found a way to let go of the heartfelt pull, which ultimately provided freedom from the burden of trying to defend our position. Jay kept his distance. Boundaries were established, and on many occasions, we all agreed to disagree.

I wish finding the balance and setting boundaries could be as easy as drawing a line in the sand or using the crime scene tape to keep the law on one side and the outlaw on the other. But that isn't reality. Family relationships can bring intricate complications to the disturbance. Everyone has personal feelings and layers of love for both the LEO couple and the outlaw. Viewpoints can be very strong, sometimes causing a family member to become a sympathizer and an enabler, which is a person who may unintentionally encourage negative or self-destructive behavior. Their perspectives can challenge the established balance and boundaries. Normal life for all those entangled can become problematic.

If an individual in your family becomes an "outlaw", it may become necessary for family members to understand clearly the role your husband has as a police officer and how you, the wife support him. The perspective you and he have, comes from his oath of office and the action steps all cops must take. Officers pursue and capture criminals, make arrests, interview victims and suspects. They then serve warrants, transfer the arrestee to jail, write the reports and testify in court. These perspectives are complex, demand respect, and earn the right to be heard.

Through communication and compromise, you can create healthy boundaries. Doing so may take time and understanding from everyone involved. Your perspective may become the most important link to establishing those healthy boundaries.

Debriefing

Jay reminds me from time to time that all outlaws are related to somebody. None of us, including you, gets to choose all the people to whom we are related or to whom our spouse is related. We can, however, choose how to respond when put in the middle of a family disturbance.

Your point of view is the "law of the land" perspective, and it can be difficult for the average person to comprehend. Police officers and their spouses understand and recognize the penal codes at a level that others may not. You understand the codification of laws related to a crime and its punishments, and you have a good understanding of the legal ramifications that can happen in a given situation. Being married to a police officer, therefore, makes your decisions firm.

Family members, in certain situations make decisions from the heart, which may be a direct conflict to the "law of the land" perspective. Therefore it is important for the family dynamic to work towards understanding, respect and finding healthy boundaries, when possible.

Bullet Points

Here are ideas and thoughts for you to explore further.

- You can love people and at the same time dislike their actions. These loved ones may be a juvenile who is just at the beginning of the journey down the criminal path or a convicted felon who is serving a life sentence for murder— or anywhere in between.
- Look for a comfortable middle ground of kindheartedness and compassion. Too much can cloud your judgment and add stress at home; too little can upset some family members.
- Harmony in the family is desirable. It may be up to you to start the difficult conversation and explain the limitations

of not being able to go beyond the boundaries. Because as a LEO he is limited, for example, to a cordial greeting at family gatherings with the "outlaw."

- Be aware that some family members may become sympathizers and enablers. This scenario can feel like you and the enabler or sympathizer are on opposite ends of a long rope, pulling and tugging to find middle ground. Neither of you may be able to understand each other's viewpoints.
- At times an intervention by outside sources such as a counselor, pastor, or a mental health professional may become necessary.
- Allow yourself grace and understanding. You and your LEO may have to walk away from the stress to avoid any further head-on collisions.
- Pray for everyone involved. I like this prayer. *Dear Lord, help us to trust you to walk beside us through times of pain and difficulty. Heal us and restore peace in us.* Say it as often as you need to do so.

Psalm 46:1 says, "God is our refuge and strength, an ever-present help in trouble."

BOLO 7

Blue Christmas

Be on the lookout for your family holiday plans to be interrupted and derailed by a real-life grinch. You may have grand plans to celebrate the holidays together, but because of his position and the responsibility to the public your husband has vowed to serve, your time together could be stolen.

WEDNESDAY, DECEMBER 23, 1987, began with fog hovering over the grounds. I could hear winter arriving as the Texas northern winds howled through the window seals. The feel of bone-chilling evenings was about to arrive. The weather forecast for the next few days included "windy, cold, and foggy with a chance of snow flurries."

Jay had been assigned to the Investigative Service Bureau in the Crimes Against Persons (CAPERS) unit as a homicide detective. He arrived home early that day from his duty, ready for a well-deserved and much welcomed extended holiday weekend. It had been years since he'd had so much time off for Christmas, and the family was thrilled. His schedule included the half-day off on Wednesday as well as Thursday through Sunday. Christmas day was on Friday, which made his holiday time off almost perfect—except for one small detail. He was on call.

Plans were in place to fill our time together with family traditions and celebrations with lots of holiday baking, feasting on turkey and dressing, and enjoying our special dessert, homemade chocolate pie. We had plenty of gift giving and receiving to enjoy and, of course, the arrival of Santa Claus. The children, ages three, five, and seven, were hyper with excitement in anticipation of the days to come and celebrating the birth of Jesus Christ. A few toys still had to be put together for Santa to place under the tree, and there were stockings to stuff and last-minute gifts to wrap. But with Jay off to help, all would be doable.

I looked around the living room and envisioned, perhaps even glimpsed, a picturesque Norman Rockwell moment. Jay was on the floor, playing with the kids. They were wearing long-sleeved flannel shirts bearing images of Santa and his elves, warm flannel pants, and socks. Jay was dressed in jeans, a white shirt, a red wool sweater, and socks. His black belt held his department issued pager, of the times, tightly to his hip.

Jay had started a tradition a few years earlier of wearing a Santa hat and a long, red, shoestring-style ribbon that dangled a jingle bell around his neck. With every move he made, the bell would jingle. The kids and Jay loved it, but to me, most days it was just another loud ringing in my ears. That night, however, it became joyful music.

The fireplace was glowing, the grandfather clock was ticking, Christmas music was playing, and the scent of hot apple cider filled the air. I took a moment to soak it all in, and then with a soft smile and a twinkle in my eye, I thought, *This looks like a normal holiday family moment!* It was a rare sight in our home, one I hoped and imagined would last all weekend.

The next morning, Christmas Eve day, we were jolted awake not by the sounds of reindeer hoofs on the rooftop but the "beep-beep-beep" of Jay's pager. He quickly made a call into the police station. Sadly, a triple homicide had taken place in Arlington. Jay, "Detective Gus," had been appointed the primary investigator of the murders. Dutifully he quickly dressed for work. His uniform as a homicide detective was plain clothes, so he chose a long-sleeved button-down shirt, black slacks, cowboy boots, a shoulder holster and gun, and a black belt to hold his pager, police radio, and handcuffs.

Before he could get out the door, the kids were awake and at his feet. Leaning down to our oldest son, he placed the Santa hat on his head and whispered, "Help your mom, please." He then looked at me and, with sorrowful eyes, placed his jingle bell around my neck.

Frowning, I thought to myself, *Gee thanks, just what I wanted.*

Jay spoke the words I had not planned for. "I don't know when I'll be home, dear. I'm sorry, kids, but I have to go to work."

With that, he hugged our two boys and picked up our daughter. She was crying crocodile tears. He gave her a bear hug and looked at me once more. "I'll call you later."

After kissing me good-bye, he grabbed his leather coat, bulletproof vest, and the keys to the unmarked detective car, which was parked in our driveway. Out into the wintery cold he went, and as the door closed, so did the possibility of another Norman Rockwell moment.

My attention quickly went to our disappointed kids. We had a long list of activities ahead for us, which I had planned for the entire family. I reminded them of our list and did the best I could to lighten the atmosphere.

I tried not to let it show, but I was *furious!* My anger was all over the place. Some was toward the situation, a small amount was directed to my husband, but mostly my anger was at the monster who had murdered people on a holiday weekend and disrupted our family's Christmas. It was a selfish way to think, I know, but the feeling was real.

I didn't have time to process compassion for the three victims who had just lost their lives or their families, who would be experiencing so much sorrow. Instead, I looked around at all I had left to do by myself and began to feel overwhelmed, not to mention disappointed about spending yet another important family holiday without my husband.

I silenced the jingle sound from the bell around my neck so I could talk softly to our kids. "Daddy has a very important job to do," I said with the best smile I could muster. "He wants me to tell you he loves you and knows you are going to enjoy spending time with your cousins today!"

The next few days of activities would include Christmas Eve with Jay's side of the family and Christmas Day with my side of the family. All of us had to "turn our frowns upside down" and, as Jay's mother would say, "get happy in the same shoes we got mad in."

Jay gave me a quick call sometime during the day and again in the evening, saying, "I still don't know when I'll be home, dear, so don't wait up for me."

I stayed up till about 1 a.m., putting the toys together and cursing at every screw that didn't fit the dang holes properly. A psychiatrist would have called my actions "misplaced anger." I thought to myself, *I'm not sure these toys were put together perfectly, but hopefully the wheels will stay on at least until Jay gets home so he can tighten the screws for me.* At the same time I wondered, *Where is he?*

For the first time since Jay had left the house that morning, my mind began to wander. My thoughts were as bone chilling as this cold wintery eve, *Dang, this guy just murdered three people! I sure hope he doesn't want to go out in a blaze of glory.* I quickly shuddered, then shook my head to clear my mind.

My next thought was, *Vicki, you don't have the time or energy to let the villain sneak in or dwell on the what-ifs.*

Whew. Self-talk-off-the-ledge success. Time for bed.

Jay slipped in quietly around 2 a.m. He fell in bed and into a deep sleep within minutes of his head hitting the pillow. At 6:30 a.m. Christmas day, when his alarm clock sounded, he rushed to get ready for work. I rushed to fix him breakfast and a sack lunch.

The sound of our voices and his intentional ringing of his jingle bell awakened the kids. One by one, they ran into the living room to see what Santa had left for them under the tree. They found their daddy dressed for work but with his Santa hat and jingle bell on.

Their excitement was contagious, and we all had a quick burst of energy. Jay stayed just long enough to enjoy their expressions and give them a kiss before leaving once again for work. At the door, he passed the Santa hat to our middle son and placed the bell around my neck once again.

Jay had told me earlier that he had no idea how many hours he would be gone or how long the case would last. Given the circumstances, I made the executive decision to allow the children to open their gifts without their dad's presence.

An arrest was made on Saturday evening, and the investigation for the District Attorney began. On Sunday, December 27, after working close to seventy-two hours nonstop, Jay returned home around four o'clock in the morning.

As for the children and me, seventy-two hours later, we had finished gift giving and receiving, singing Christmas carols, reading Jesus' birth story, eating turkey and dressing and, of course, the family favorite chocolate pie. We were in the process of cleaning up from the long three days of celebrating with family and friends.

Jay had missed it all.

While our kids were dreaming of the arrival of Santa, my husband had spent his holiday time at a grim crime scene where innocent people, including a four-month-old child, lost their lives.

I hadn't thought much about what Jay was doing after he left our house on Christmas Eve. I was too deep into our family activities. As difficult as it was for us to be without him for the holiday celebrations, I now realize it must have been even more so for him to witness the violent truth of the triple homicide crime scene. I guess, as the wife of a police officer who had become a homicide detective, I had blocked out earlier what was unpleasant.

On Christmas Eve and the days that followed, I instead had thought about what was in front of me: three precious children in anticipation of the holiday events and an overwhelming amount of work to be done. The jingle bell necklace reminded me Jay was at work as did his empty seat, once again, at our Christmas dinner table. Of course, I had saved leftovers of his favorite foods, but when the time came, he was too tired to enjoy them.

I didn't ask Jay too many questions about the case that weekend or in the weeks that followed. Maybe it was partially because of the age of our children and how busy I was. Maybe I didn't care because I was angry. Or maybe I just didn't want to know the gory details of a triple homicide that included a four-month-old baby. However, I knew the main reason was that when Jay finally returned home, I was physically and emotionally worn out and he was exhausted. He crawled into bed and slept for hours. When he awoke, the family showered him with Christmas gifts and included him in what was left of our not-so-normal holiday.

The case made headlines: The murderer had gone on a killing spree on December 24, and a total of four, not three people, were dead. He had shot three adult males to death in two different locations and a four-month-old baby boy was also a victim. Three of those innocent lives, including the baby, were lost in Arlington. The fourth victim's life was taken away in Fort Worth.

As for the murderer, he was apprehended in a motel in Fort Worth by the Fort Worth Special Weapons and Tactics (SWAT) team. The cbsnews.com site reported, "Police found a sawed-off shotgun, two pistols, a flare gun, ammunition, and blasting caps in the man's motel room after he was arrested." The Fort Worth *Star Telegram* reported that he had said he wanted to "kill a bunch of people" and that he would shoot police officers. As I had feared, he also had said he wanted to go out in a blaze of glory.

In the days ahead, Jay and his partner, along with a detective from Fort Worth, worked together tirelessly to bring this evil man to justice. I was told later that during his capital murder trial in 1991, the perpetrator grabbed a loaded gun from a drawer in the courtroom in an attempt to kill the judge. He was wrestled to the ground, and no one was injured. Eventually he was sentenced to death row. On March 14, 2017, he was executed. Justice was served at last.

Yes, our Christmas was blue without Jay, however knowing he helped apprehend this 'real-life grinch", which ultimately saved many lives was a comfort. Most of all, I was relieved to have Jay home safe and sound. I took the jingle bell from around my neck and placed it around his, where it belonged. The intense three days had past. Now it was our turn, as a family to take a deep breath, relax and enjoy celebrating on our own (typical) belated LEO holiday schedule.

Debriefing

That year was without a doubt my hardest Christmas holiday of being married to a police officer. I will never forget December 24 and the days that followed. I will never forget the disappointment and furious feeling I had toward this murderer who took so many lives and derailed our family's holiday celebration.

Not once, however, did I think to put on my imaginary bulletproof vest to protect my heart. Instead I allowed the disappointment to get the best of me, at least for the first twelve hours of the seventy-two-hour experience.

Did I cope with this well? Some would say probably not. I had learned the hard way that crime scenes, confessions, and arrests didn't recognize holidays. As Jay says, "Real crimes are not solved in sixty minutes like they are on TV."

Was I naïve to think that an on-call CAPERS homicide detective actually could enjoy the holidays without interruption? Yes. I could not think like a monster, so I could never have imagined someone would be so evil, especially on Christmas Eve. Also, the number of homicides in the 1980s in Arlington was only between five and eight a year, so I had no reason to anticipate this type of holiday derailment.

Did I have an action plan in place, just in case Jay got called into work? No. I believe this was my biggest mistake, which added unnecessary stress to an already stress-filled season. My expectation of our holiday had been polar opposite to our reality. I let the entire situation personally affect my world in a negative way. Looking back, I say nothing should have that much power.

Jay says I handled it better than I'm giving myself credit for. "Vicki, you kept the kids happy, fed me when I was home, and allowed me to get the rest I needed to do my job."

Someone special said to me, "His expectations were far more realistic."

Although I chose to share our "Blue Christmas" story with you, please keep in mind that celebrations of *any occasion* could be derailed because of his badge. It may be a simple gathering with friends your family holiday plans or a special milestone celebration.

So how can you keep from falling victim when you find yourself in a similar situation?

Bullet Points

Here's my ammunition of advice.

- Expect the unexpected, and play the "what-if" game ahead of time. Try not to be a victim by falling into a situation similar to ours.
- Look both ways. Be prepared in advance, think like a cop, and have a contingency plan in place. Had I planned in advance for him to be called in for work, I would not have been as disappointed, frustrated, and angry. I could have thought to myself, *Okay, plan B. I'm used to this! We can do this, kids, and mom is ready!*
- Give yourself grace. Anger and disappointment are normal human emotions. Sometimes we need a little extra help to control them.
- Remember to give your LEO grace. You will need to understand and respect their dedication and duty bound responsibility to

the department and the community they serve. This will allow you to keep your challenges, disappointments and frustrations in perspective.

- Second Corinthians 12:9 says, "My grace is sufficient for you, for my power is made perfect in weakness. Therefore I will boast all the more gladly about my weaknesses, so that Christ's power may rest on me."
- Take time during busy seasons such as Christmas and Thanksgiving to pray for a peaceful heart.

John 14:27 says, "Peace I leave with you; my peace I give you. I do not give to you as the world gives. Do not let your hearts be troubled and do not be afraid."

BOLO **8**

My Daddy Is a Real Policeman

Be on the lookout for your family to have a unique set of challenges. Jay calls them "miscellaneous incidents." These incidents can be scheduling issues, family rules, or unusual conversations. For one thing, raising children in a law enforcement home has an additional layer of safety procedures and an instinctive overprotectiveness by one or both parents. As they grow up, your children might go through several stages of feelings, from pride to embarrassment, because their daddy is a "real policeman."

RAISING CHILDREN WITH A cop for a daddy is quite a different experience for LEO families compared to other families outside of our Blue Nation. Jay and I discovered that the safety standards and family rules he and I established were often perceived as overbearingly restrictive in the eyes of our children and sometimes our extended family and friends. They were, however, necessary in our minds. After all, our kids' daddy had way too many miscellaneous incidents at work.

In case you are wondering, a miscellaneous incident is when an officer is called to help someone but discovers no offense has occurred. For example, two family members have a disagreement. One of them decides to call the police. A disagreement is not an offense, so the officer fills out a "Number 5," or a miscellaneous incident report.

I would say our family has had its own fair share of personal miscellaneous incidents, *no form required*. Many of them occurred because of their daddy's badge. This chapter is filled with a variety of my favorite stories of raising children in a LEO home. They may give you a look at what's ahead for your family or a laugh over what's behind!

Family Cuteness and Pride

Jay was at the beginning of his second year on the police force when our oldest son was born, and we proceeded to have three kids in four years. Our boys were twenty months apart, and our daughter was born right after our oldest son's fourth birthday. As you can imagine, family life was very busy. While I mastered the art of nursing, Jay became a master at diaper changing and bath time. I can't imagine how many diapers we went through during those years.

So how were we different from other families during those years? Here is an example that happened right at the very beginning: our first child's birth announcement was a BOLO! Here is how my husband showed his creativity.

> *ALL UNITS: BE ON THE LOOKOUT. White/Male 7 lbs., 2 oz. 19" tall. Brown hair, blue eyes. Date of birth 7-8-80 @ 3:49 p.m. Released from the hospital in the company of proud parents Jay and Vicki. WANTED: for being cute and cuddly. Should be wearing a clean diaper. M.O.: Will be eating, sleeping, or crying.*

We, or I should say *he,* wasn't nearly as creative the next time around. Our second child was born breach, and I needed an emergency C-section. With Jay's rotating shift schedule and little time off, a twenty-month-old, a newborn, and my recovery (*whew!*), our second son's birth announcement came low on the to-do list. We managed, however, by the age of two, to take an extremely cute picture of him, proudly wearing a police uniform, just his size.

By the time our third child arrived, we were far too busy to even think about being creative. Even photos were difficult to accomplish. It would have been nice to have the technology of cell phones with cameras back in the 1980s. Our daughter asked us so many times why there were so few pictures of her that we settled on one simple response: "The camera broke."

My favorite miscellaneous incident about our daughter is dripping in cuteness. I can still visualize the incident as if it happened yesterday. It occurred on an occasion when Jay was dressed in uniform to work a part-time job. For the first few years of our daughter's life, he had worked in plain clothes. Every once in a while, however, he worked a part-time job that required his uniform.

One day after Jay finished getting dressed, he walked into the living room to kiss everyone good-bye. The boys and I didn't think anything of it, but our four-year-old daughter was amazed! She jumped to her feet in awe.

Wide-eyed with excitement and with pride in her voice (as much as a four-year-old could express), she ran to him and exclaimed, "Wow! My daddy is a policeman, a *real* policeman!" He instinctively picked her up and bear hugged her. The beam in their eyes showed the kind of unconditional love that only a LEO daddy and his daughter could share. For me, it was a priceless moment, and it made all the sacrifices of our life because of his badge worthwhile.

One particular photo of our daughter, which we did fortunately take and somehow found the time to get it developed, was from a father-daughter dance when she was ten years old. Jay was working his shift during the scheduled event, but he managed to stop by, in uniform, just in the nick of time to dance with her. I don't know if it was a priceless moment for her, but it was for him.

These miscellaneous incidents in her life must have made a very big impression on our little girl. She now has a degree in criminal justice and is married to a police officer. She and her husband are raising two precious boys who are less than two years apart, just as our first two children. The standard good-bye of these boys when their daddy leaves for work is similar to what ours was. Everyone gets a kiss, the words "I love you," is never a missed moment, and as he's walking out the door, someone always says, "Stay safe, Daddy."

Safety First

Safety was always a top priority in our family. I'm sure it is in most LEO families. For us, however, everything, and I really mean everything, had an *extra* layer of safety rules attached. The safety procedure "Look both ways before you cross the street" applied; however, it was heightened to "And be aware of your surroundings at all times." Doing so became instinctive to all of us.

Driving had its own set of requirements as well. All of us knew what it meant to drive safely, and we knew how to pick out the safest parking spot. Was it close to the door? Did it have good lighting? What type of car was parked next to it? Would it be better in this place to park head in or to back in?

Here's another thing about cars. Have you discovered the safest way to get your children in and out of a car is to open just one door and let them climb in and out? Who knew? Oh, we did!

Everyone these days know "stranger, danger." This rule and many more like it became imbedded in our kids' minds. They all boiled down to one: "Kids, trust no one." Of course, Jay made it clear to them that if they were ever in danger, scared, or lost, they were to look either for someone in a uniform or a mother with children.

Shopping was always a challenge because of our safety rules. I would tell Jay where I wanted to go, only to hear the comment, "No, you can't go to *that* store! It has been robbed more than once recently." Sometimes, if the kids and I were lucky, we could take our armed guard, *aka* Daddy, with us.

Oh, I love this next one. I got a call one day from Jay while he was at work, and he said, "You and the kids are never going to the mall again!"

Seriously?

"Sorry, honey, but that one is just impossible to follow," I replied, telling him we would talk about it when he got home. We learned to compromise on a few of his more outrageous safety requests.

Safety in numbers is always a good rule, unless you are at a public park, Jay drilled into us. Even I began to think everyone looked like a pedophile. I found myself watching not only my children but also everyone else's children, even if I didn't know them. This instinct also kicked in at parties, pools, sporting events, and actually just about everywhere I went without Jay. I had a hard time relaxing because it felt as if I were the only adult watching the children.

You may be wondering how we handled play dates and sleepovers. Good question. We had to know the family well enough to trust them with our child. Sadly, we came to realize that we could count the number of trusted families on one hand for all three children.

Everyone, of course, was welcome to our home. My question was always, *Would they want to come over a second time?* Some kids and their parents didn't like our house rules. Any play guns were "checked" at the front door because all guns in our home were real. That fact, of course, also came with its own set of safety rules.

If the kids or I wanted to jog on the street, especially by ourselves, we would hear the response from Jay, "Are you crazy? No way!" No exceptions or compromise ever happened on that one.

If another teenager wanted to drive one of our teenagers to a party, the answer was always a big, fat no. They could drive their own car. That way, if the party escalated to an unsafe level, they could leave.

I could go on and on about the overly protective safety rules, but I think you get the gist (and jest) of it.

Family Mealtime

A big challenge in our family was finding the time to have meals together. Jay's shift schedule and our kids' awake time or school time were often in direct conflict with each other. The part-time jobs he picked up on his days off limited our mealtime togetherness too. Also, during most of his career, we didn't have the luxury of living in the same area of Jay's beat, so he couldn't come home for meals.

Jay and I decided to make a commitment to our family and figure out a way to sit down for a meal with Daddy at least once, if not twice, during his workweek. Taking three small children anywhere in public, was an experience in itself, but to stay true to our family time meal commitment, we did it anyway.

To accomplish this task, we had to be willing to be creative and somewhat vulnerable. Our favorite place to meet became the local cafeteria. The kids liked it, they would eat well, and it was affordable. I would be able to show up at the agreed upon time with our three kids, hoping their daddy would be able to join us. Seventy percent of the time he'd arrive somewhat on time. Thirty percent of the time, he was either late or a no show. When he arrived in uniform, he attracted stares from everyone. After a while, we didn't care and became used to it.

Whenever we dined out, Jay carried policeman pal badges and his personal police trading cards to give to other children who were dining in the restaurant. When he first arrived, he or our children would hand younger children the policeman pal badge, which was a gold sticker in the shape of his APD badge. It said, "Policeman Pal, Arlington Police Department." It was complete with a star in the center. The trading cards went to the older children, which Jay thought encouraged integrity. By doing so, Jay felt he could help break the cycle of children growing up afraid of cops. Our kids loved doing this for their daddy.

After the policeman pal badges and trading cards were passed out, we'd find a table where Jay could face the front door. A booth was too restricting for him. He was always on heightened alert and ready for just about anything. Once seated, he'd place his police radio on the table and turned it up so he could listen, attracting even more attention. Sometimes he wore his earpiece, but he learned that amongst the chaos of three kids wanting his attention at once, me asking how his shift was going, and listening to his radio, it just seemed easier for him to place it on the table.

Many times, in the middle of a bite or sentence, he would simply stand up and say, "Gotta go. Bye." In a blink of an eye, the kids and I were left alone while Daddy rushed to his next call. His abrupt departures were disappointing.

I won't deny it. Those times were difficult, but we got used to it.

Twenty Minutes of Quality Time

We lived twenty minutes from everything, including our kids' school and church. When Jay worked the evening shift, I would insist he drive the kids to school at least once or twice a week. That way he could have his quality time with them. Because our children spent most of their time at school and then after-school sports or church, sometimes Jay's morning drive time with them would be the only time they would see each other for several days.

This twenty-minute quality time drive was valuable to Jay, so he used it wisely. The radio was off, and the conversations flowed based on what was happening in life at that moment. Jay and I labeled these times, "Dad's teachable moments." I'm sure our kids would have called them "oh, brother, rolling of the eyes moments."

Every once in a while, Jay's creative scheduling allowed him to take his Signal 40 (lunch break) at the perfect time and place where the kids were practicing a sport. He would score extra points with them whenever he could swing by during one of their games. Those occasions were a win for everyone.

Our middle son told me a while back, "I thought Dad was present for everything! He knew what was going on in my life, and was interested, especially when it came to sports." Apparently those check-in times Jay worked into his day were well worth the effort.

"Dad, don't embarrass me!"

Here's a funny story that easily could have been an actual miscellaneous incident. Our oldest son, who was in the fifth grade at the time, had forgotten his backpack for school. I was already at work, so I called Jay and asked if he could drop it off. At that time, Jay was the Vice Sergeant, working undercover. He was driving a beat-up truck, and I would say his appearance was sloppy, at best.

Jay arrived at the school and parked the truck. He proceeded to walk toward the school grounds with backpack in tow. Terrible timing, because the school just had a "potential" bomb threat. The officials were using their safety procedures for an evacuation. All the elementary students were lined up outside the building, which was the school's protocol during the 1990s.

When a school official and many of the students noticed a "suspicious man" carrying a backpack who was about to enter the building, the School Resource Officer (SRO) was notified. He immediately went into action. Fortunately, when the SRO approached Jay, he recognized him. The SRO then assured the school officials that there was nothing to be concerned about. It was just Sergeant Gus, bringing his son the forgotten backpack, he told them. Jay then was told where he could find his son, who was totally embarrassed by all the unwanted attention and the way his daddy looked that day. He never forgot his backpack again.

Most children are embarrassed by their parents from time to time and for one reason or another. Having a LEO as a parent adds a unique category of embarrassment for them and sometimes also an added label: "tattle-tale." Wendy Burgess's daughter Brittany experienced both the embarrassment and the label.

"Her stepfather is Constable Clint Burgess. His position as a Constable is an elected position; therefore, he is well known in Tarrant County," Wendy told me.

"After we moved Brittany from a private school to public school in the ninth grade, she quickly discovered, as she was meeting new friends, how uncomfortable she was about sharing that her stepdad was a law enforcement officer. Her fear was that she would be instantly labeled the school 'snitch or tattle-tale.' It wasn't until she became friends with her new acquaintances and trust developed between them that she felt comfortable to share who her stepfather was."

I can imagine how difficult that situation must have been for Brittany and for other LEO children who face this challenge. Our kids didn't experience this particular issue because everyone already knew what their daddy did for a living. During their high school years when they met others outside their environment, however, they too had to assess the situation and relationship before disclosing the fact that their dad was a cop.

Other Teachable Moments

When our oldest was fifteen years old, we moved to an area more convenient to school and church. Jay could even come home for meals from time to time too. That was a blessing.

About that time, our two boys were old enough to become curious about the police gear on Jay's uniform. One day he decided to describe what the items were and why he carried them. When he got to the handcuffs, he thought they were old enough to take part in a "hands on" show and tell. Before they knew it, one of them was handcuffed. This teachable moment showed them that they never wanted to find themselves wearing those "metal bracelets." Jay then jokingly said, "Oh, sorry. I left my handcuff keys at work." Freak out moment for them!

In their later years of high school, the boys and their friends began to ask Jay all kinds of police questions. He usually responded by answering their questions using real-life stories, sometimes putting the fear in them. He ended those conversations by saying, "Boys, situations like the one you just asked about will get you in big boy jail. So don't do it."

One day Jay brought home a briefcase filled with examples of all the different street drugs on the market to show at a neighborhood watch program. He showed the drugs to the parents and then later to our children. He described what each one was. This teachable moment was a clear message to our kids that Daddy knew everything about everything. (It wasn't true, but they didn't know it.)

When our boys began to go out on the weekends with their friends, I would notice Jay using his interrogation skills on them. I would come to their rescue, laugh, and say, "Jay, quit interrogating the children."

Jay would shrug his shoulders and then say to them, "Okay, boys. No drugs, no knives, no alcohol, or premarital sex. Have a good time and be home by eleven-thirty." They would just roll their eyes, but it showed us they were listening.

Our kids were far from perfect, including their driving skills. Each one of them at one time or another was pulled over for speeding. Jay would get a courtesy call from the officer letting him know how fast his son or daughter was driving and the location. Each time Jay made them write an apology letter to the officer. They were also grounded.

The boys learned that they could use their dad as an excuse to decline participating in certain gatherings or parties where underage, illegal activities were happening. There was, however, one time when our daughter didn't use this excuse as she should have. The result was alarming.

The miscellaneous incident happened at the beginning of the school year. Our daughter was sixteen at the time. One evening I became suspicious that she wasn't telling me the truth about her plans. This concern prompted me to begin my own investigation. I called around and found out our daughter was with her friends at Dan's house. She did not have our permission to be there.

When Jay arrived home from work, I told him where she was. We both decided to get our daughter out of this home. He quickly changed from his uniform to street clothes.

We drove to the home and saw our daughter's car, along with many other cars, parked on the street. There were teenagers everywhere. Jay got out of the car and walked to the door. He told me later, "When Dan answered the door and the kids saw who it was, the place went silent."

"I am here to get my daughter," Jay told Dan. "Where is she?"

Dan pointed, but word spread quickly because our daughter came promptly on her own.

I know Jay must have looked at her with his stern, police-like stare. As she walked behind him toward the car, I could hear her saying, "Dad, please don't say anything. Just. Keep. Walking."

He honored her request.

I drove our daughter home in our car that night, and Jay took her car. Once home, the three of us had a deep conversation about her actions, the party, and how quickly it could have gotten out of hand.

To her credit, our daughter took the time to reflect on her actions. Eventually the embarrassment and being mortified for disobeying our rules wore off. She called us into her room and said, "Mom and Dad, thank you. No other parent would have done what you did. Now my friends know not to invite me again." We were glad she had learned her lesson and greatly appreciated her apology, but she was still grounded.

One Surreal Scene

Our boys spent a lot of time at our church's Methodist Youth Fellowship (MYF) on Sunday evenings. Jay, *aka* Sergeant Gus, volunteered to coordinate a community service program for the MYF group with the organization Mothers Against Drunk Driving (MADD). One evening Sergeant Gus and another officer, along with the MADD representatives brought to church a trailer that carried the actual Arlington patrol unit in which two officers had died. On one side of the trailer were poster-sized pictures of officers Terry Lewis and Jerry Crocker, along with the story of their families and their service.

Sergeant Gus and the officer created a setting as if it were an actual crime scene. The yellow crime scene tape was placed around the trailer, along with flares and orange cones. Patrol cars were positioned on both sides of the trailer, their headlights aimed directly at the crumpled car. The sun had gone down for the evening, so the patrol cars' overhead red flashing lights created quite a powerful scene. Members of the youth group, the sponsors, and some parents, including me, gathered around the crime scene.

Sergeant Gus, his officer, and the MADD representatives began their presentation. As they were sharing information about the officers and how a drunk driver killed them, suddenly a wave of emotion came over me. I could barely take it all in. I looked around this surreal scene and unexpectedly a lump filled my throat and then a chill ran down my spine. The tears weren't far behind.

I looked at my husband as he spoke about these officers. Then I looked over at the mangled patrol car. My eyes turned to our two boys, ages thirteen and fifteen. They were listening intently as their daddy spoke. As I stood there looking at this graphic visual image, my mothering instincts suddenly rose to the surface. I closed my eyes for a moment, perhaps to hold back the tears. When I opened my eyes, I imagined our two boys at the age of three and five. I wanted to run over there and protect them from what they were seeing and hearing.

I wondered what they were thinking at that moment, but I knew what I was thinking: *Could this happen to their daddy? Will my husband's picture and story someday take the place of what I was seeing and hearing?*

The presentation ended, and we were encouraged to get a closer look at the crushed patrol car and spend time reading about the families. I remember feeling as if my feet were glued to the cement. I couldn't move toward the wreckage or read the officers' stories, so I walked away. As I did, the tears began to roll down my cheeks. I said a prayer for the families and thanked God that it wasn't Jay's story.

To most of those who were in the audience, the event was simply the message of the week for MYF: "Do not drink and drive." By the next day, they would have forgotten most of it and returned to the busyness of their lives. To me it was so much more. It felt personal. I needed my personal, imaginary bulletproof vest to protect my heart and allow me to take a deep breath and send the villain away.

I took the boys home and asked them what their thoughts were. Reality kicked back in as they said, "Oh, it was cool. Don't worry,

Mom. We won't drink and drive." I could hear how proud they were that their dad was a policeman. There was no indication in their voices of *my fear.*

Jay finished his shift and returned home around midnight. I told him they all did a great job and our boys received their message loud and clear. I did not mention to him the effect this program had on me. I was just glad to give him a big hug and hold him extra tight.

The MADD program would empower me in the days ahead with the inspiration to write my poem, "Coffee and Donuts: A Tribute to My Husband." Some of the adults who were with me that night also attended the Bible study at church where I presented my poem for the first time as the weekly devotional.

This excerpt shows how that MADD presentation affected my heart and life:

> I was reminded last week of the death of two cops,
> Killed by a drunk driver—and I think my heart stopped.
> I couldn't read about them, it bothered me so,
> That their families are without them
> Yet their children would still grow.
>
> As I walked away with tears down my cheek,
> I shuddered to think, *Could this happen to him?*
> It wasn't just coffee and donuts for them.
> And now our hearts slowly mend.

Debriefing

Raising children is challenging for most parents regardless of what they do for a living. It's difficult to be a hands-on, active parent and find the balance to allow growth and independence without smothering kids. As a LEO family, you will more than likely mix in your own extra layer of safety rules and police-related, teachable moments just as we did.

You may have heard the saying, "It takes a village to raise children." I truly believe it does. Our church helped us raise our children. We required them to be active in Sunday school, youth choir, summer camps, MYF, and mission trips. The messages they heard were cohesive with our family values, rules, and guidelines. We tried our best to instill a moral compass in our children so when they did waiver, we prayed, this compass would help them make the right decisions. Proverbs 22:6 says, "Start children off on the way they should go, and even when they are old they will not turn from it."

Don't misunderstand. Our kids had their fair share of growing pains, rebellion, defiance, and mishaps. Jay and I were also far from perfect parents. We made a fair number of mistakes as we parented though the difficulties that came our way. We tried to keep Christ as the center of our decisions.

Our children are now grown adults. They all have college degrees and their own careers. Incidentally, they all considered law enforcement, but none of them chose to pursue it as a career. However, as I mentioned earlier, our son-in-law is a police officer. We have a wonderful relationship with all our kids and their spouses and are blessed with five beautiful and smart grandchildren.

Bullet Points

Here are some ideas to consider as you raise your children in a law enforcement home.

- Be proud of your husband, and your kids will notice and hopefully have the same feeling for their dad.
- If a child of yours is embarrassed or labeled the "school snitch," it's important to have the lines of communication open between you and the child and if necessary, the school administration.

- Understand the value of your husband's request to have his family follow an extra layer of safety rules. You and his family are the most important people in his universe. He wants you to be safe.

- Do your best not to let paranoia get in the way of raising your children.

- Be careful not to project your greatest fears onto your children. They don't need the burden of your worries.

- If your children show signs of being afraid for their father, assess the situation and take action based on their age, their concern, and their understanding. Sometimes reassurance is all they need. Seek professional help if your child doesn't show signs of improving.

- Some officers have a difficult time leaving their authoritative tone and attitude at work. At times, they can be short-tempered with the children, stern and unapproachable. Jay struggled finding the balance from time to time as well. Of course he always meant well, but there were occasions when I had to remind him to tone it down a notch (or two). Usually this loving nudge worked wonders.

- Assess the importance of family time versus the concern of being seen in public with your LEO. As a couple, evaluate this decision based on the community you live in and what his position is within the department.

- Be a proactive police family in your community. Participate and plan safety related programs at your children's schools, your church, and your neighborhood.

Be comforted by this Scripture verse: "When Jesus saw this, he was indignant. He said to them, 'Let the little children come to me, and do not hinder them, for the kingdom of God belongs to such as these'" Mark 10:14.

BOLO 9

"Do" Process

Be on the lookout for an impending process. Law enforcement has a process for everything, including a "mental process" that your husband and you will inevitably go through. Most people have a natural compassion for humankind. This will not allow the mental process to be ignored.

AS WE ALL KNOW, police officers are dispatched for service to a variety of calls. Every day officers have the potential of receiving calls to something unique. This reality is, in part, the thrill of their job. But police officers also have an established order, or process, for everything. Police departments outline them in their General Orders, (GO) and Standard Operating Procedures (SOP). The mental process, however, is unwritten.

Prior to responding to a call or making a traffic stop, for example, officers are trained to process in their mind a variety of possibilities that might happen. Jay says, "These are the *what-ifs* of police work, meaning officers have to think in advance how they will handle a situation if the traffic stop or dispatched call escalates or isn't exactly 'routine' based on the information given."

The unspoken process officers don't often talk about is the emotional, mental process that takes place after handling certain calls. Some officers assume they are immune to this process because they are "tough." This assumption is sometimes referred to as the "John Wayne Syndrome," meaning they think they can handle anything. The *New York Times* says these John Wayne types "often keep their feelings to themselves or attempt to deal with their problems alone."

Corporal Billy Seals, a forty-five-year police veteran who dedicated most of his career to the officer training division, told me, "For a new officer, it takes a few times to learn how to mentally process events most people will never see. It is common for new officers, as soon as they leave a difficult call, to 'break down' before they start to process what just took place. They then begin to ask themselves, *Am I cut out for this job? Am I too weak or not strong enough, to handle this line of work?* It's really just human emotion. Over time, hopefully, they will figure out how to work though their personal mental processing."

Jay says, "Some calls make everyone involved stop and wonder, how do we make sense of what we just saw, heard, or felt?"

Some real-life stories require police officers as well as their wives to engage in a deeper mental process before they can put it to rest, and the following was one of those calls.

It happened on a Friday night in October. Jay was the patrol sergeant assigned to the east side of town. Our two teenage boys were spending the night with friends, and our daughter was upstairs in her room, sound asleep.

I have always been a night owl, so it wasn't unusual for me to be awake when Jay arrived home. That night I was in bed already, attempting to catch up on my sleep. I didn't often fall into the deep sleep we all hope to reach quickly once our head hits the pillow—at least not until Jay was home safe. That night I was in one of my typical "sleeping with one ear and one eye open" sleep patterns I had grown accustomed to, especially since Jay and I had two busy teenagers in our lives. My ear was tuned toward the direction of the garage, waiting for the sound of the garage door to open and close.

At last my ear heard the sound I was waiting for. Jay had arrived home from his 3 p.m. to 11 p.m. shift, or so I thought. I glanced at the clock with my one-eye-opened eye and noticed it was 1 a.m., much later than his usual arrival time. I immediately tuned both ears toward the kitchen, waiting for him to reach into the refrigerator for something to drink. All I heard was silence.

Hum, I thought to myself. *Maybe I was in a deeper sleep than I thought and just missed the refrigerator sound.* I stayed in bed for a few more minutes, hoping to hear the sound of Velcro ripping apart as he took off his ballistic vest.

No sound. Just silence.

Okay, I thought, *maybe he needs his space. No, maybe he needs to talk. Does he need my support right now? Did he get a chance to eat? Hum.*

I never know quite what to do when all I hear is silence, so I decided right then that the sound of silence was one of the most thought-provoking sounds my husband, the police officer, could make.

I rolled out of bed and walked to the kitchen. There he was, unusually quiet, and I could see the sadness in his eyes. I could tell that he was tired and emotionally drained. Eventually I spoke to break the silence, asking him if he'd had a chance to eat.

"No," he said quietly. "I'm not hungry."

Without asking, I reached into the refrigerator and pulled out a Dr. Pepper for him. I then began to fix him two grilled cheese sandwiches because I knew he was hungry, he just didn't know it at this moment. He sat down at the breakfast table, still fully dressed in his uniform.

"Why don't you go change while I finish making you something to eat," I said.

When he returned to the kitchen, he seemed a bit more relaxed than what he had looked like a few minutes ago; however, the sadness in his eyes was still present. He scarfed down the sandwiches and began to unwind.

My usual lighthearted question when he arrived home from work was, "How was your day?" But that night, I decided to be a bit more specific, so I asked him, "Hey, honey, what kept you working late tonight?"

With a slow-to-respond answer and sorrow in his voice, he said, "A death investigation."

"Oh, I'm sorry, honey. Who died?"

I could tell when he looked up at me and then hesitated to continue that he wasn't sure if he wanted to share this particular call with me. So I got up from the table and took two beers out of the refrigerator, one for him and one for me. It was my nonverbal communication to him that I was awake and ready to listen.

Once more I asked, "Who died?"

Slowly and methodically, Jay began to share what had happened, but he avoided the answer to my question. He'd do that a lot. I'd ask him a question, and he'd go into a long, lengthy, roundabout way of explanation before finally disclosing the answer. This night was no different.

Silently I thought to myself, *I'm glad he's at least begun to verbalize the event that took place.* I'd learned through experience from the fifteen years he'd been on the police force that verbalizing was a safe way for him to start mentally processing what had taken place.

"I was dispatched to a convenience store where a homeless man had been dumpster diving," he said.

My mind immediately began to visualize an older man and what he might have looked like, digging into the nasty dumpster for his next meal. Jay didn't go into details of the appearance of this homeless man, so my mind went directly to the stereotypical malnourished, hungry, and filthy from head to toe conceptual image. I could imagine unmanaged hair and facial features drawn from sadness and a difficult life.

All at once, compassion began to fill my heart, and then sadness swept over me as I began to process what Jay was sharing. I, at that moment, had gathered my own suspicions of what might have taken place next, and I secretly hoped my thoughts were wrong.

Jay continued. I swallowed deeply.

The "dumpster diver," as Jay persisted in calling him, had found what he thought was a whole chicken wrapped up in a black plastic trash bag. When he tore opened the bag, however, what he saw was not what he'd expected. He went inside the convenience store and told the manager, "There is something that looks wrong in a black bag in the dumpster. Can you please call 9–1–1?"

Jay was the first to arrive on scene and start the process of interviewing the manager and dumpster diver, who were both waiting outside. "We all walked over to the dumpster together," Jay said. "Then I opened the sliding door to see, officially, what was inside."

He stopped talking for a moment, and I could tell he was collecting his thoughts. He took a couple of sips of beer before continuing and then said, "The dumpster was almost full to capacity with trash, and the smell was horrific."

As he spoke those words, instinctively he shook his head. I could tell he was trying to shake off the memory of the awful stench that was still fresh in his mind. Of course, my creative imagination went directly to flies and insects busily finding their way in and out of the dumpster. Jay continued to describe to me the nasty scene as I visualized the three men, waving their hands intermittently to avoid personal contact with the pesky bugs.

Jay said, "I used my flashlight to help me see what all was inside the dumpster. I then discovered, as the dumpster diver had described, a partly torn open bag with what appeared to be a deceased newborn baby inside."

My stomach instantly felt ill, as Jay had confirmed my secret suspicion with the truth. He had finally disclosed the answer to my question about who had died. It was a newborn baby.

"Oh my God, Jay!" I blurted out immediately with a churning mixture of emotions. Then I followed up with a livid comment. "What kind of mother would throw her baby away in a dumpster?"

Jay responded in his official way by acknowledging, "We don't know yet. This case is now in the hands of a homicide detective."

Both of us then, not just him, had to mentally process what he had experienced. Jay was at the tail end of his processing, but I was at the beginning of mine. My heart began to ache for this poor, innocent baby who was literally thrown away with the trash. Jay instinctively consoled me.

I created a mental checklist to begin helping me through the process while my mind continued to ping pong back and forth between compassion and anger. It was something I'd learned to do years ago to help me process the stories Jay shared that were especially difficult. I was saddened for the hungry and homeless man, but my heart was just breaking for the innocent baby. I had a mixture of emotions for Jay and everyone who was involved, but mostly I was bewildered by the actions of the mother.

What was going through this mother's mind when she threw her baby in the dumpster? I wondered. *Did she personally put her baby in a plastic bag and in the dumpster? Was she glad, as in good riddance? Or did she cry for the loss of this baby?*

More sadness swept over me as I wondered if this mother was a victim herself at the hands of an angry man. It was a lot to process, and I was personally glad I hadn't been there to see the unthinkable crime scene. My creative imagination was sufficient enough.

I asked Jay to tell me more. He continued by sharing what actions he and his officers took next. "There was a lot to process," he said. Many procedures had to take place before he could complete, or as officers say, "clear this call." He had to contact the homicide unit, crime scene investigators, fire department and ambulance service, the assistant police chief, and the medical examiner.

Jay then described in detail how he and his officers handled the crime scene itself. "A number of police, the media, and bystanders began to show up. It was nighttime, so the emergency lights quickly drew a crowd. There were people around the scene crying and out of control. In disbelief, everyone began to realize it was a horrible tragedy."

It was Jay, *aka* Sgt. Gus, who was responsible for protecting the crime scene. He cordoned it off and assigned officers to all sides to protect the area and control the crowd. The fire and ambulance crews were quickly released from the scene, and then the homicide and crime scene units arrived to perform their duties of collecting evidence.

"A representative from the medical examiner's office arrived, verified the remains, and determined it to be a deceased human, an African American baby girl that appeared to be stillborn." Jay said.

An angel foundation (a group of volunteers who provide burial services for babies and children when no one claims the deceased) had already heard of the incident and sent a representative to meet Sgt. Gus and the medical examiner at the scene. The foundation representative blessed the innocent baby girl with a name, Lily, like the flower. After the blessing of the name, the medical examiner removed the baby from the scene.

When Jay spoke of the foundation rep giving her a name, a chill of happiness ran through my body. *God has already "processed" this baby into heaven and into the loving arms of Jesus,* I told myself.

"I cleared," Jay said at last, meaning he had completed the required process for the call and was able to come home. But as this story shows, he still had the mental process work to do in the hours and maybe days ahead.

If you ask your husband, you will probably hear something like what Jay reminded me of the next day. "As a police officer, I have to work past being stunned about what I see. I tell myself, like I've done my entire career, this is my job, and I will do it professionally. I am the authority in each situation and need to take charge of this investigation as a first responder. Remain calm while everything else around me is chaos. People become hysterical at tragic events. When I get home, then it's my time to process what took place and the role I had in it."

When I asked Jay what he bottled up inside the most, he said, "Signal 18 calls, which are death investigations. Especially calls with infants and children who died. Those are the calls that are slow to process. Some are much harder to process than others."

Like all officers, Jay must be on the lookout for the necessary processes related to a crime scene, whether they are formally written down by the department or just known by seasoned officers. For each call, Jay says, "There is an unofficial, four-step process. First, process the situation, and then process the scene and what's happening at the scene. Eventually process it in a report. Then after it's all over, it's the officer's turn to process how it affects him emotionally."

Department requirements vary, but Jay says, "Some have special debriefings or after-action reports following certain critical incidents to assure that the officers involved go through the steps necessary to process what they saw and experienced."

Officer Robert recently experienced one of his department's required debriefings after a domestic violence call ended with the death of a suspect. The suspect had threatened his family and the police, stolen a car, and attempted to barricade himself in a stranger's home. When they arrived on the scene, Robert and several other officers, including a member of the SWAT team, found themselves looking down the barrel of their rifles at the suspect with their sights on the man's forehead.

Robert didn't have to take the shot, but he and the other officers witnessed a member of the SWAT team shoot the man. Robert said, "The suspect put the lives of many innocent people at risk that day. Fortunately, no citizens or officers were hurt by the suspect. This was the first shooting many officers on scene had ever been a part of, so they found it difficult to process what had actually taken place. Less than a week later a debriefing was held, which helped the newer officers mentally deal with the incident and provided a bit of closure."

Because processing such an event is something LEOWs must do as well, I spoke with JoAnne, Robert's wife, and asked her, "What is the most difficult scenario you ever had to process?"

"The July 7, 2016, Dallas Police shootings where five officers were assassinated during a peaceful march!" she said without hesitation. "That was difficult, and it happened not long after Robert hit the streets. I could feel fear and anxiety building up inside of me, and for weeks it was hard to watch him leave for work. I remember going to a memorial at the police station right after it happened with some other police wives, and we prayed. Some of us had trouble putting our prayers into words, but to have the instant support of other police wives, some I had just met, was a blessing. We were all trying to process what took place."

What she said next was, "It wasn't just a local hurt. I have police wife friends in other states who were experiencing the same feelings. We all leaned on each other while we processed everything."

JoAnne then shared her very personal struggle to process. "The state of our country and the public view of police officers at the time layered on more things that I needed to process. I think everyone, police wives and citizens alike, had to process this particular tragedy. I learned that processing takes time, but with prayer and a good support system, I made it through.

It's important to be able to process to the end and be able to come out the other side," she added. "I'll never forget the brave men who lost their lives, and I will never forget how it made me feel. That, by far, was the most difficult situation I have had to process as a police wife."

Debriefing

You and I live with law enforcement officers who see evil "up close and personal." Our husbands know firsthand that evil is entangled throughout our cities. When these officers, whom we love so dearly, are face to face with people who have no compassion for humanity or are filled with pure evil in their hearts, we can't help but be affected too.

I had a rose-colored-glasses view of the world when Jay became a police officer. However, I've listened and learned how to process his real-life stories. Over time, I was forced to remove those rose-colored glasses. Even though I wasn't personally present at any crime scene, I will never be able to completely erase from my mind some stories Jay shared with me as he mentally processed them. Most importantly, however, they have been processed.

Do process. Closure is so important, and the best form of closure is to create and go through your own personal, mental processing system.

Bullet Points

Here are some of my suggestions for you.

- Starting a conversation with your husband can be difficult at times. He may not want to share with you about certain calls or experiences, wanting to protect you from having to go through the process too. Communication is vital through the tough times—for both him and you—so take the initiative if he doesn't.
- He may or may not ever tell you all the details, and that's okay.
- It can take hours, days, or weeks to process certain calls or experiences.
- There is a fine line between TMI and NEI. Communication will help you define what level you are both comfortable with. With each experience, I learned I was "brave enough." That's all I needed to be.
- You might not want to hear the details or that his life was in danger in fear that you won't be able to handle it. In times like these, you can lean on this verse of Scripture: "So do not fear, for I am with you; do not be dismayed, for I am your God. I will strengthen you and help you; I will uphold you with my righteous right hand" (Isaiah 41:10).
- You are your LEO's most important support system. Corporal Billy Seals, as an FTO, said, "Police officers need a support system at home. Someone who is willing to offer their support

and understanding. I have trained rookies who would make excellent police officers but didn't have the support from their spouse, so eventually they would turn in their badge. Also, if their spouse or support system is constantly asking, "What did you do?" instead of, "How was your day?" and probing for all the daily details, it won't be long before the spouse asks him to leave the force."

- Pay attention to his nonverbal communication. All of us have our own way of handling the stress and how we process certain things.

    Is he quiet or distant?
    Does he begin to drink alcohol or more alcohol frequently?
    Is he having trouble sleeping or relaxing after work?
    Is his mind someplace else?
    Is he short-tempered?

- If any of those stress symptoms get a strong hold on either of you, consider seeking professional help.

I end this chapter with Jay's favorite Bible verse: "But those who hope in the LORD will renew their strength. They will soar on wings like eagles; they will run and not grow weary, they will walk and not be faint" (Isaiah 40:31).

BOLO 10

"Altered" Egos

Be on the lookout for "altered" egos to surface in a fun way. Law enforcement officers feel they are constantly being watched and scrutinized with every move they make. From time to time, they just want to alter their LEO persona and have fun. Also, many officers work their shifts with increased adrenaline rushing through their bodies, so it is no surprise that their hobby choices also might have a heightened amount of excitement. As your husband's life partner, you too can get into the fun and thrill of his "altered" ego.

JAY ONCE WAS AN adrenaline junkie, both on the job and at home. In the 1980s, his adrenaline-filled hobby was participating in all-police rodeos. A decade later, he moved to a Harley Davidson. A few years ago, he bought his dream car, a shiny black Corvette. The thrills and spills that have happened as he enjoyed these hobbies have been like a roller-coaster ride for me. I've had to hold on tight, close my eyes, and pray for survival on many occasions.

The rootin'-tootin', mud-slinging, yee-ha, western style, all-police rodeo was by far the most thrilling hobby Jay engaged in, and it was something the entire family could enjoy. Participants in the wild and crazy Texas Police Officer Rodeo Association (TPORA) rodeos were required to be commissioned law enforcement officers in the State of Texas or the wife or daughter of an officer. Our local group, the Arlington Police Rodeo Team (APRT), consisted of patrol officers, FTOs, sergeants, lieutenants, detectives, motor jocks (motorcycle officers), wives, and daughters along with other weekend warrior cowboys from the APD who joined in the fun from time to time.

I asked Jay's friend Gary Shipp recently why he joined the APRT team back in the day, and he said, "I wanted to do something fun with our daughter. She loved horses and was an avid barrel racer." For the uninitiated, a barrel-racing event is where a horse and rider attempt to complete a cloverleaf pattern around three preset barrels in the fastest time.

Gary also said to me, "By the way, this was the only police group I was ever with where work never came up. It was relaxing to me. I'm an adrenaline junkie, and I miss the thrill of it all."

That statement was no surprise to me or his wife, Mary, who shook her head in agreement.

I laughed and thought, *Wow, that was relaxing? The rodeo events he and Jay participated in stressed me out just watching them!*

Like Gary, Jay found thrill and relaxation in the rodeos. He pursued his hobby so much so that he even became the president of APRT and held the position for a few years. The APRT participated on average in seven rodeos a year, which were held about every other weekend during rodeo season throughout the state of Texas. The APRT also hosted a few rodeos, raising money for the John Peter Smith Hospital Pediatric Clinic Pharmacy Fund.

For most rodeos, around two hundred or so police officers from across the state would take off their bulletproof vests and put on a western style vest. These cops, I mean cowboys, would put their life on the line for a chance to win a shiny, gold plated, oversized trophy belt buckle by competing in one or more of the events. (If you've never been to one of these rodeos, you might be surprised to learn that people from near and far come to watch their local law enforcement officers show their cowboy skills.)

The cop "cowboys" participated in bull riding, bareback riding, chute dogging (steer wrestling), team roping, the wild horse race, and two-man calf tie (calf roping) events. The "cowgirls" participated in goat tying and barrel racing. There was even a calf scramble for the kids!

Have you ever seen a wild horse race? If not, you are in luck, because I reserved you a front row seat for this wild and crazy rodeo event. Imagine you are with us in real time. Are you ready?

In the spring of 1984, Jay and I packed our Dodge Ram with boots, belts, and cowboy hats for the whole family. After buckling in our two boys, ages two and three, we headed south for another fun-filled weekend in Austin, Texas.

Our first stop was at the McDonald's in Alvarado, where we "42'd" (met up) with our APRT friends. Next, before heading out, we confirmed that everyone was on the same CB (citizen's band) channel. "Radio check," Billy would say, and then the designated CB operator in each vehicle would respond, in order, with a "10-4, good buddy" (understood).

Our caravan included six law-abiding, gun-toting cowboys (law enforcement officers). Three of them were hauling two-horse trailers. Since I was pregnant that year, the caravan agreed to add an extra restroom stop to the four-hour drive to Austin.

Once we were ENRT (in route), we headed southbound on Interstate 35, which in the 1980s was a two-lane (each direction) divided highway with a national required speed limit of only fifty-five MPH (today it's three lanes and eighty MPH). About an hour into our trip, our "incognito cops" began to get restless as they watched the rest of the traffic speed by them at seventy MPH or more. When someone tried to pass all six of our vehicles recklessly and irresponsibly, our cowboys, I mean cops, decided it was time to take control of the speeding traffic. One of them got on the CB and broadcast two words: "traffic control." In a split second, in sync, all six pick-up trucks positioned into a formation that limited other vehicles from passing them, including the reckless driver.

Let me paint this picture for you a little clearer. Imagine six pick-up trucks, three of them pulling horse trailers, staggered side by side, driving *exactly* the speed limit. They continued this journey assignment they unofficially called "Operation Escort" for many miles.

Oh, and then it got even better. Another familiar voice on the CB said, "Shift." Just like that, in sync, all six vehicles switched lanes into their new positions. These traffic-controlling cowboy cops repeated this pattern over and over. The result was that the road ahead of us was clear but the traffic behind us, stretching about halfway back to the McDonald's, had no choice but to go the posted speed limit of fifty-five MPH.

When our officers determined that Operation Escort mission was accomplished, they announced that it was time for a restroom break. We pulled off, in sync again, at a rest area. The travelers behind us must have been ecstatic.

According to Jay, it was just "a random act of helpfulness to control the traffic."

Seriously, guys? I thought to myself. *It was their outlandish cop humor, but I bet all the others traveling on the interstate with us said they were "a real pain" or worse. But that's okay, these cowboy cops are used to being called names.*

In just the allotted time for the trip, our caravan arrived at the host hotel for this TPORA rodeo. Everyone settled in. Jay and the boys took a quick nap, thank goodness. I was fidgety and uncomfortable because baby number three was due to arrive in a few months.

After naptime, I watched Jay transform into his "altered" ego, a real-life cowboy. He put on his favorite pair of Wrangler brand jeans and then brown leather chaps for better protection. After buttoning on and tucking in the tails of his APRT maroon team-colored monogramed shirt, he put on his cowboy vest. He then tied a maroon folded bandana around his neck.

Next he reached for his cowhide leather gloves and stuffed them into a back pocket for safekeeping. He then added silver spurs to his almost worn-out cowboy boots and put on his summertime Stetson, a natural straw cowboy hat. He finished off his outfit by proudly buckling on the shiny first place trophy belt buckle he'd won at the previous month's rodeo. His initials, JMG, were etched on the back of his western style belt. I dressed our two precious cowboys to look like their daddy, which included their initials on the back of their western style belts.

When everyone was ready, our cowboy family met up with the rest of our APRT members at the arena. They had saved us, including you, seats. It was a good thing they'd arrived early because the stands were packed full of rodeo fans. I'd wrangled together a few snacks and toys for the occasion, just in case, but my little cowboys were entertained just fine by watching the rodeo.

Jay was slotted for two events: the wild horse race, which consisted of three team members, and the two-man calf tie. Based on the schedule of that night's performances, the wild horse race was about midway through the evening, and the calf tie was toward the end. As each event was completed and the time drew closer for the wild horse race, my adrenaline kicked in. I began to get antsy in anticipation of Jay's wild horse race.

At last four of the rodeo chutes began to fill with untamed wild horses, each with only a halter and a lead rope. I could hear and see these wild creatures snort, raise their heads, rear up, and kick with all their might as they resisted being restrained in the chutes. They wouldn't be in there long. Four teams of three cowboys each had gathered in the arena and were positioning themselves close to the chute to hold their draw of a wild horse.

Each team member had a very important duty to perform. One would hold the lead rope, one would "mug" the horse, and the third would saddle the untamed beast and attempt to ride it across the finish line. Of course, the fastest team to accomplish the goal within the two-minute time frame would win the three coveted first place trophy belt buckles.

In theory it sounds easy, right?

Jay is handed the lead rope, and soon I hear resistance sounds from his wild horse. The mugger, Keith, is in perfect position to perform his mugging duty of distracting the horse by grabbing ahold of its ears and twisting them. Gary, the rider, then places his homemade saddle on the ground and puts his hand on the chute gate. Our APRT wild horse race team members are now in position, waiting with anticipation for the bullhorn to sound. My heart is racing, and my two little cowboys are anxious and excited to watch their daddy in the arena.

The bullhorn blows, and Gary slowly opens the chute gate to let the wild horse out. Jay holds tight to the lead rope with all his might in an attempt to manhandle this wild beast just long enough for Keith to leap up, grab ahold of the horse's head, and start twisting its ears. Gary, the ultimate adrenaline junkie on this team, grabs his saddle and moves into position, close enough to the horse to throw his saddle on, cinch it tight, and then jump on and ride to the finish line, which is at the far south end of the arena.

Sounds thrilling, right?

A few times, the wild horse race actually happened as I described. That night, however, from what I could see through my fingers partially covering my eyes, a bunch of macho police officer cowboys were being pushed and dragged around the arena like rag dolls.

Our team's wild horse forced Jay and Keith to be sandwiched for a few moments between it and two other wild horses that by then were running free because their team ropers had lost grip on the lead ropes. These two free running wild horses were kicking and stomping on anything or anybody they happened to run into, in their effort to escape.

Their lead rope cowboys moved in close, with the hope of grabbing ahold of the lead ropes again. Chaos was all around, and the clock had less than one minute to go before the buzzer sounded.

Jay's horse knocked him to the ground. Jay, thinking he was as strong as this horse, refused to let go of the rope. I glanced through my fingers once more, just in time to see him being dragged across the arena. He was face down, arms straight out, but holding on tightly to the lead rope of the wild beast. Someone, at that moment, captured the scene perfectly on a camera.

Keith, the mugger, ran to catch up to Jay and the beast. When he did, he attempted to mug the horse. By this time, the horse was way out of control and showed its fury. The second attempt to mug it failed. It was clear that these guys really wanted a trophy buckle. They were not about to give up like two other teams already had, not until the sound of the buzzer.

At this point in time, Jay is standing up again and holding tight to the lead rope. Keith tries once again to hold onto the horse's head and ears. Success! The horse finally stops fighting back. I see Gary through my fingers, which are almost glued to my face at this point. I see him saddle the horse, which is now facing north, and climb onto the saddle and begin to ride.

Oh, but wait! The finish line is the other way! My boys and I scream in excitement and relief as Gary turns the horse around and crosses the finish line just ahead of the sound of the buzzer. These extremely confident and courageous cowboys have made a very thrilling event for everyone, especially those of us sitting on the front row!

Jay brushes off as much dirt and manure as he can before he returns to where the boys and I are seated. He laughs as he sits down and says, "That was fun! I literally understand what one horsepower really is."

I hand him a beer and shake my head in disbelief and relief that he is okay. *I'm used to it, I guess*, I think to myself.

The next event is the two-man calf tie and yes, Jay holds the rope. But this time it's only for a calf. Billy runs down the rope and ties. The rodeo ends, and our wild horse team members each take home a trophy belt buckle to add to their growing collection.

They try to convince me this evening was relaxing and fun. I think they are crazy. What about you? You might say it was exciting and entertaining! At the very least, I hope you enjoyed the coveted front row seats.

Typically these occasions end with a dance under the stars. That night our two young cowboys were tired and so was I, so we skipped the dance, but just that once.

Nine years flew by as our family took part in this adrenaline rush hobby. Jay received and recovered fully from a few broken ribs, a dislocated shoulder, and many bumps and bruises.

Not long after he stopped the rodeo hobby, Jay traded his Stetson for a motorcycle helmet. He was thrilled to purchase a previously owned white, Harley Davidson Road King, police-equipped motorcycle from one of the motor sergeants. Riding it became his new, "altered" ego way of getting away from the stressful trials of police work and, as I would say, "Just being Jay for the day."

I'd never been on a motorcycle before, and to tell you the truth, I was nervous about this new adventure. When he was on the rodeo team, all I did was ride shotgun in his truck and then watch him perform. Climbing onto that motorcycle with him took me to a whole new level of adrenaline rush.

Eight hours a day, Jay drove a patrol car; and as we know, almost everyone moves out of a police officer's way. So it was no surprise that he became a pro at weaving in, out, and around traffic, able to reach his destinations safely and in record time. Jay drove his civilian car somewhat the same way. He came to forget that he didn't have flashing lights on top. He expected the traffic to part, like the Red Sea, just for him!

Needless to say, I wasn't looking forward to weaving in and out of traffic on a motorcycle with him at seventy to eighty MPH. After all, I didn't and still don't have an "altered" ego like him. This motorcycle thing stretched my risk-taking skills to the max.

Thankfully Jay had decided to learn from the best. After his civilian motorcycle training, he participated in a police officer motors unit training course. In no time, he was a pro at driving his Harley.

Somehow he convinced me it was time for me to enjoy this new adventure. We went shopping again, for me this time. After all, if I was going to embrace this new adventure, I needed to do it in style and become a fashionista gal on a motorcycle!

My prayer life increased with each new ride, especially the ones where sharp curves, high winds, and rain were involved. I found myself holding on tight, closing my eyes, and staying in contact with the man up above. For his part, Jay liked keeping up with the high-risk, adrenaline junkie crowd on "bikes." It wasn't long before he traded in his Road King for a brand new, blue Ultra Classic Electra Glide, Peace Officer Special Edition. I must say it was a much improved and comfortable ride. We added speakers and microphones to our helmets. Cool!

You might be interested to know that Jay's new "altered" ego "incognito cop uniform" consisted of Wrangler brand jeans, motorcycle chaps (black leather), black gloves with finger holes for the summertime, solid and insulated ones for the colder months, a team vest or black leather bomber style jacket, a black helmet, and black motorcycle Harley boots. Of course, his off-duty Glock was secured somewhere on his person.

We eventually became members of three different motorcycle clubs: the local chapter of BKTX1 (Blue Knights International, Law Enforcement Motorcycle Club), our local H.O.G. (Harley Owners Group) club, and the UMME (United Methodist Motorcycle Enthusiast) club. Depending on what shift Jay worked in any given week, we could be active with one of those groups.

Jay felt most comfortable with Blue Knights, a nationwide group exclusive to active and retired law enforcement officers and their spouses. We attended their dinner meetings, and before long he was voted in as Sergeant at Arms. We hosted and participated in local events and ones in other cities as well to raise money for several charities. As we participated in these events, Jay collected ride pins for his vests.

Poker runs were the popular rides, and they were tons of fun! A poker run had five stops along designated back roads. With each stop, the driver drew a card. At the end of the ride, the driver with the best poker hand from the five cards he or she drew won the prize. We never won, but we helped raise money for important causes by participating.

Our time with the Harley came to an end after I broke both my ankles stepping into a Texas-size 18" sloped curb-style storm drain. It was a very difficult recovery, which took around eighteen months. After the recovery period, these rides were no longer enjoyable to me. Jay rode from time to time without me, but eventually he sold his bike in 2009, which, by the way, helped pay for our daughter's wedding.

A few years ago, Jay's lifelong dream of owning a Corvette came true. He purchased a previously owned C6 2008 black-on-black coupe and quickly joined the Panther City Corvette Club for active or retired law enforcement officers and their spouses.

We now enjoy traveling around the countryside on four wheels, with the top off, allowing the freedom of the wind to swirl around us. Jay, now in his sixties, takes *almost* age-appropriate risks. I still find myself closing my eyes around sharp curves and praying for our safety.

I continue to thank God for the opportunity to now enjoy Jay's "unaltered" ego and our (slower) "mini" roller-coaster life.

Debriefing

This chapter lets you know how my LEO husband found ways to escape the stress from his duties and relax in ways that were fun for him. My hope is that it will help you see and understand your husband's need for activities that complement his "altered" ego. His stress outlets may look very different from Jay's.

Although my husband's choices seemed a bit risky and required an adrenaline rush, they were so much fun for him and me. We also loved the opportunities they brought to raise funds for charities, which is important to us.

I'm sure wherever you live there is something your husband could participate in, either with other officers or by himself. If you are willing to participate in his chosen stress-releasing activities, it can be a fun way to stay connected with him. I love the saying, "A family that plays together, stays together."

Bullet Points

Here are some thoughts to help you embrace whatever "altered" ego your husband chooses.

- Some officers enjoy the freedom of game hunting out in the wild.
- Others enjoy spending time at the shooting range, mastering their skills and reloading their own bullets.
- Our friend Gary, after his rodeo days, purchased a speedboat and spent his extra time on the lake and at his beach house on the Gulf of Mexico.
- Robert and Jimmy choose to feed their adrenaline rush through physical fitness. They spend a lot of their extra time at the gym.
- Robert also enjoys riding his mountain bike. He said, "I like going to state parks. I enjoy the surroundings of nature. Most times I ride hard and use this as a cardio workout."
- A former police officer for the APD, now retired, took his physical fitness to the max and became Mr. Olympia.
- Police Olympics, team sports, leagues, and other competitive activities help relieve stress.
- Some officers go the opposite way to relieve their stress and choose mind-releasing activities such as fishing, bowling, or reading.
- Other LEOs invite friends over for cookouts and let the kids run around or relax and watch sports in their man cave.

- If your husband isn't currently active in a hobby, you might pray he finds something fun to do with fellow officers, you, and your family. As I like to say now, looking back, "We didn't know we were making memories. We just knew we were having fun."
- You might find an opportunity to support a good cause and enjoy making memories. Jay found a way for us to give to others in need that brought us personal satisfaction.

The Bible tells us, "Each of you should give what you have decided in your heart to give, not reluctantly or under compulsion, for God loves a cheerful giver." 2 Corinthians 9:7.

BOLO 11

Gremlins aka Pitfalls

Be on the lookout for "gremlins" that grab ahold of and destroy the passion and spirit of your spouse! These gremlins are also known as the pitfalls of police work. They come in many forms, have varying powers, and can cling to their target anytime during a law enforcement officer's career. The good news is that once your spouse and you get a visual on a gremlin, a positive resolution is possible.

WHEN MY HUSBAND AND I were dating, one of our favorite places to go was a drive-in movie theater. One weekend we watched two slapstick comedies by Mel Brooks, *Young Frankenstein* and *Silent Movie*. We laughed until our sides ached, more importantly at the same silly lines! As our relationship developed and we began spending most of our free moments together, I noticed how funny Jay was and how often he made me laugh. I fell in love with his quick thinking, corny one-liners, and dry sense of humor.

After we were married and he became a police officer, Jay continued to be light-hearted and easygoing. I could tell he loved life and his job. The inner, boy-like excitement was present. He would gear up for work with enthusiasm, ready to tackle whatever crossed his path.

As years passed, Jay's light-hearted demeanor began to fade. It became noticeable, especially when he would gear up for work. By the time he finished strapping on his gun and badge and then dug deep inside for his daily dose of courage, he had transformed into the very serious Sergeant Gus.

Seriously! Where did his humor go? I'd ask myself.

I used to jokingly say to him, "Someday I'm going to write a book on how you change from happy-go-lucky Jay to serious Sergeant Gus."

Sometimes I'd even question him in a good-humored sort of way, hoping to help him snap out of this gloomy state of mind.

"Hello! Jay? Are you here?"

He'd snap back at me with one of his "oh-so-serious" looks and reply, "That's not funny, Vicki."

I would laugh to myself and snap back at him, "Well, one of us needs to lighten up around here!"

It was meant to be a simple reminder to him that he was taking life way too seriously.

I was disheartened to see Jay losing part of himself, the light-hearted personality that God gave him. I worried how long this gremlin would hang around and keep ahold of him. Did life as a police officer really have to be so serious?

I began to miss him, even when we were together.

On one hand, I understood the role of a police officer was serious. For example, he had the ability to take people's freedom away when they broke the law. That act, in itself, was a huge responsibility. On the other hand, you may recall in the introduction of *His Badge, My Story* I spoke of the nonmandatory but highly recommended meeting for police spouses, and at this meeting the sharing couple said, "It is common for police officers to experience the pitfall of becoming very serious."

Looking back, I remember thinking, *what a bummer, I can't imagine Jay losing his sense of humor!*

Little did I know that this gremlin would become his greatest foe.

Jay's gremlin I called "too serious" rode on his back off and on for years. It was difficult for me to watch, knowing it had such a strong hold on his humor, forcing him to be way too serious. This gremlin wasn't going to let go without a struggle.

There were times when Jay was quiet, withdrawn, and had restless nights. I could see the tense emotion in his eyes as he relived the sadness and dangers of his assignments. The weight of the job and his compassion for the victims and his fellow officers who were hurt or lost their lives mounted up, hindering his ability to relax and have fun.

God bless him, I would think to myself, and sometimes I would even say, "I'm here for you. Jay, just breathe." Other times, I would find myself frustrated, losing my patience, and sometimes angry about the situation.

When he finally recognized what was happening to him, he began to battle with the gremlin "too serious," only to recognize it had given birth to a few more named, "stress" and "balance." He then had to learn to balance the stress from work to be himself at home. Although he tried, he couldn't leave his work at the office. However, he could choose to have fun and knock the gremlins off his back.

Long-time friends Mary and Gary Shipp were celebrating fifty years together at the time I was writing this book. Gary had earned a bachelor's degree in criminal justice with a minor in psychology. In 1997 he'd retired as Deputy Chief, 2nd in Command, for the Arlington Police Department. Mary had been my hairdresser for many years. You may recall in BOLO 10: "Altered" Egos that Gary and Mary had one daughter who was an avid barrel racer.

When I asked Gary if he experienced any pitfalls during his career, he laughed and said, "Yep. Just about every one of them!" He listed them for me by memory, one by one. I looked down at my list of pitfalls and thought, *Wow, he really did hit most of them!*

Mary smiled, shook her head, and said, "Yes, I agree. He went through just about all them."

Gary was quite familiar with isolation. He said, "Throughout my twenty-nine-year career on the police force I had a hard time relaxing and letting go when I was with people outside the law enforcement community. I learned early in my career that I was better suited to have friends inside the police community." Both Mary and Gary were content with that decision. Gary continued with, "As I rose in the ranks of the police department, isolation was just part of the journey."

Gary shared one story with me that happened early in his career. It helped him and Mary realize they had to tackle the gremlin of isolation together. Their neighborhood was hosting a gathering, and to be social, they decided to attend. Gary was concerned about going but decided it would be a good way to meet the neighbors. However, in case things went badly, he and Mary made an agreement in advance. "I told Mary if things don't go well, we will just leave," he said. She agreed.

It wasn't long before one of the neighbors came up to Gary and started criticizing and bashing police officers and the department. "I could see Gary was in an intense conversation with the neighbor," Mary said. "He was trying to keep his cool and restrain himself, but the situation was beginning to escalate. I recognized Gary needed a way to walk away from the confrontation and just go home." She got his attention, and they left the gathering, disappointed.

Distance and sometimes separation from neighbors became inevitable for this couple. What I gleaned from their story was that they were prepared in advance and had an action plan in place, just in case something happened. Even a simple neighborhood gathering required Gary to take a "police style" approach with the neighbors, refraining from negative interactions.

The good news was that Gary discovered he could have social connections on the inside of the department. He and Mary enjoyed spending time with other couples they met through his journey with the APD. Even today, they still enjoy their weekly bowling league.

In a phone call with Kimberley Salinas, a police wife and friend, the conversation turned from discussing our weekly Bible study for LEOWs to her husband's experiences with gremlins. She and Jimmy have been married for over twenty years and have two children. Jimmy is still on the force, and currently he is the sergeant over the APD training academy. He's been with the department for over thirty years and has held several different positions throughout his career.

Kimberley told me that Jimmy's gremlin is his tendency to be overly suspicious of people. She said, "He is aware of everything that goes on around him, regardless of where we are or what we are doing. It's hard for him to relax when he senses something is not right."

I totally understand, having felt at times the same gremlin clinging to Jay.

She continued. "He sees the worst of the worst and deals with the dark side of everything. For his sake and mine, I try to be the flip side of that coin. I feel my role is to offer balance. I love him so much that everything else is just fluff."

Kimberley recognized she needn't put too much weight on the small things.

Most everyone in law enforcement or married to an officer, hopefully will eventually understand what triggers a gremlin for them, but some are able to deal with their gremlins more effectively than others. Here is a great example of a solution once you recognize your LEO is facing a gremlin.

Corporal Billy Seals was assigned to the southeast side of town because of his temperament and ability to talk to people. His superiors continued to ask him to stay there because of the excellent work he was doing. Janet, Billy's wife, said, "And he did, and he did, and he did. He worked this district longer than any other officer."

Over time, Janet noticed his temperament at home was becoming cynical. "I told him it was time to 'bid out' of that district. He finally agreed, thank God. After he changed to a different side of town, he returned to the man I knew he was and loved. He needed me to let him know it was time for a change. I'm sure he recognized it too since he didn't stay there."

Janet acknowledged Billy needed a change. As an avid barrel racer, she had to keep the three barrels standing up and balanced to win the race. The three barrels symbolized her life, his life, and their life together.

Attitudes are chosen ways to respond to stimuli. Chronic suspicion can manifest itself as a cynical attitude. Overseriousness can show up as an authoritative attitude. In an article that appeared in *Law and Order Magazine* in 2014, Beth Sanborn, a veteran of Pennsylvania's the Lower Gwynedd Police Department and an instructor at Delaware Valley College, said, "Police officers are accustomed to calling the shots. They are accustomed to getting their way." Many officers develop a need to be in charge that can sometimes be unhealthy.

It took about a decade for Jay's authoritative attitude to slip into our home. At first I tried to blow it off. *Okay*, I'd think to myself, *he does this all day.* At work he's a "just the facts, ma'am" guy in a *Dragnet* sort of way. In other words, he doesn't need to know the entire story, just the facts. Sometimes his attitude would lead me to think, *maybe he had a tough case, call or arrest, so I'll give him a break and let this time go.*

At some point, however, I noticed his "command presence" had finally become overbearing to me and the kids. I found it necessary to put on my imaginary bulletproof vest and, in my own *Dragnet* sort of way, present him with "just the facts, sir."

Jay was not the only one in our family who had to figure out how to conquer gremlins. I had to learn to cope with and fend them off whenever they attacked him. More than once, with a deep breath, I'd put my hand out like a cop and say, "STOP!" (It was meant to be a reenactment of what he had done several times, instinctively, to me.)

Next I said something like, "Honey, your command presence at home is overbearing. I have seen the palm of your hand too many times. We don't live by your standard operating procedures (SOP) in our home, so please stop issuing me orders and start asking me nicely."

He'd look at me, then smile and say, "I'm sorry, dear."

I'd smile back and add, "Oh, and one more thing. Quit interrogating our kids."

"I will try, I promise," he'd say.

We'd both take a deep breath and give each other a big hug.

"Relax, Jay," I'd say. "You're at home, and we love you."

Numerous times throughout his career, it was necessary for me to remind him that I was his wife and deserved a different attitude and approach than what he had used on the arrestee just a few hours ago.

Melissa Littles, a published author, blogger, and advocate for law enforcement officers and their families, once said, "Being the wife of a police officer is not for the weak; or the self-centered; or the needy, clingy, insecure, or high maintenance type of woman." I wholeheartedly agree with her.

However, we must also recognize we have our own LEOW gremlins to be aware of. If you find yourself face-to-face with one or more of these creatures, there is comfort in knowing these gremlins can be caged.

Debriefing

To begin confronting gremlins, *aka* pitfalls, you first need to recognize them and accept the fact that they do occur. It is unfortunate, but they are common in the world of law enforcement. In my opinion, they are not signs of weakness. They are a side effect to the longevity of seeing and experiencing what law enforcement officers face day after day. You and your spouse more than likely will experience one or more of them sometime during his career.

What follows are some examples of Law Enforcement Officers pitfalls, *aka* gremlins. It will be helpful for you to become familiar with them.

GREMLINS LAW ENFORCEMENT OFFICERS MAY FACE

ON THE JOB:

- Takes everything too seriously.
- Difficulty associating with others outside the profession.
- Becomes cynical, arrogant, negative, or all three.
- Trust issues and chronic suspicion.
- Loses sight of his core values.
- Faces an unpredictable work schedule.
- Works too many part-time jobs.
- Doesn't handle complaints professionally.
- Doesn't agree with disciplinary actions.
- Experiences disappointment from not getting a promotion.
- Feels like he or she has been falsely accused.
- Internal Affairs issues.

AT HOME:

- Is hyper-vigilant; can't relax.
- Seems unable to balance work and home life.
- Isolates himself.
- Feels that family life can tend to be boring or mundane.
- Has a high expectation of his family members, including his children.
- Is overly protective of his family members.
- Has an ultra-authoritative attitude, overly harsh on the spouse and family.
- Feels like he's on duty 24/7.
- Feels his job is more important than family matters.
- Challenged in communication with balancing TMI and NEI.
- Doesn't think his spouse understands him.
- Has an affair.
- Thinks about divorce.

EMOTIONAL AND HEALTH ISSUES:

- Neglects his spiritual life.
- Suppresses emotions.
- Poor sleep habits.
- Becomes bitter, frustrated and negative.
- Turns to others besides his spouse for emotional support.
- Has alcohol or drug related problems.
- Develops high blood pressure or gains excessive weight.
- Struggles with depression.
- Shows signs of post-traumatic stress disorder (PTSD).
- Thoughts of suicide.

GREMLINS WIVES OF LAW ENFORCEMENT OFFICERS MAY FACE

HOME AND FAMILY ISSUES:

- Develops trust issues toward her husband.
- Becomes overly protective.
- Poor sleep habits.
- Can't find the balance.
- Doesn't like his unpredictable work schedule.
- Has an affair.
- Thinks about divorce.

EMOTIONAL & HEALTH ISSUES:

- Worries excessively.
- Experiences anxiety and fear.
- Suppresses emotions.
- Develops resentment toward the job and assignments.
- Feels the effects of isolation and loneliness.
- Chronic suspicion.
- Becomes bitter or negative, like her husband.

- Feels misunderstood.
- Develops high blood pressure or gains excessive weight.
- Neglects her spiritual life.

If one or more of the LEO gremlins is affecting your husband and they seem overwhelming, then he may need time to decompress. This line of work actually has a title for decompressing. It is called "the chair." It refers LEOs to that special place they like to go to unwind or just sit in silence.

After a particularly rough shift at work, Jay would sit on the back porch alone and process the experience of the day, on some occasions turning it over to God in prayer. Sometimes he would go for a ride on his Harley or work out with his weights to clear his head. After he had processed his situation, sometimes he would share what he felt comfortable sharing with me.

Take heart. Life is good, and these gremlins can be "arrested." So just breathe and come up with a plan.

Bullet Points

Here is an attack plan Jay and I have learned, based on our experience, for tackling the gremlins.

- Read this chapter together.
- Educate yourself on the pitfalls.
- Recognize and accept them for what they are.
- Communicate with each other.
- Know you are not alone.
- Call your healthcare provider and ask for references that are covered under your insurance; seek help.
- Seek help from other resources, and if needed, get professional help in the law enforcement field.
- The chaplain of your husband's department is a good resource. He or she can guide you to the help needed based on the

pitfalls you or your spouse are facing. His department may have other resources.

- Many books have been written on the topic as well that you might find helpful. Check on Amazon or Google. Key words suggestions are: Law Enforcement Pitfalls, Law Enforcement Survival.
- Lean on the strength of our Lord to help with gremlins.

Psalm 118:13–14 says, "I was pushed back and about to fall, but the LORD helped me. The LORD is my strength and my defense; he has become my salvation."

BOLO 12

Balancing Act

Be on the lookout for courage and confidence to stay balanced. You may feel sometimes as if you are on a narrow LEOW balance beam, trying to keep your life balanced and well-adjusted between the world of law enforcement and the rest of society.

A s I mentioned in the BOLO 5: Guard Your Heart, my friend Angela and I took gymnastics together when we were younger. Angela was fearless on the vault, uneven bars, and balance beam. I was self-conscious and cautious, which limited my ability to push myself as a gymnast. Sometimes the 4-foot high, 16-foot 5-inch long by 4-inch wide balance beam seemed twice as long and half as wide. From time to time, it felt like the beam tilted right or left.

During exercise routines, gymnasts are expected to maintain balance and grace while performing dance and acrobatic moves on the beam. The best gymnasts attack the beam with courage, confidence, flexibility, and power. Each 90-second gymnast's routine is performed in front of an audience and judges. Routines have to cover the entire length of the beam and include acrobatic moves. At the end of each routine, the gymnast is to leave the balance beam and land on solid ground, poised and standing proud. It takes practice, discipline, and concentration.

During U.S.A. Olympic gymnastics performances, the audience is on the sidelines. On one side of the gymnasium, fans cheer as they watch the routines being performed, holding up signs to show their support and proudly chanting, "U.S.A., U.S.A!" On the other side, the audience watches in silence or sometimes stern disapproval. Hateful signs and comments are occasionally used to show dislike for our country and what it stands for.

A LEOWs life may seem at times to be played out in a gymnasium on a special beam I call the "LEOW balance beam." The performances require mental and emotional skills not unlike those of gymnasts, all watched carefully by an audience as well.

On one side of the gymnasium stands a crowd of our Blue Nation. It consists of uniformed officers, other police wives, and proud supporters. These spectators stand for all that is right and good in law enforcement. They hold up signs saying, "courage, strength, and honor." LEOWs among them who are not performing show their support by displaying thin blue-line banners and flags.

On the other side of the gymnasium is a mixed crowd of family members, coworkers, friends, and others. These spectators represent to the performers where they live, work, and worship; where their children's schools and community activities are; and where girlfriends reside. A handful of this crowd shows support with reserved cheers, and a sparse number of thin blue-line flags scattered around.

Sadly, spread across this crowd are also displays of negativity. Several people even show hatred with signs and banners that are hurtful. Some shout out harsh words, which are captured in songs such as "Cop Killer."

Where are the law enforcement officer wives who are ready to perform? Right in the middle of the gymnasium in front of that special LEOW balance beam, lined up for their turn at attempting to balance life with a cop and life in their community.

The LEOW balancing act isn't easy. Like a gymnast's act, it takes people trained and experienced in handling the routine. The LEOWs need courage, confidence, flexibility, and strength. On occasion, they feel acutely that they are being watched and judged.

The LEOW role is unique, and so is our performance. We are expected to show our ability with incredible stunts on the beam, all the while holding a tray of coffee and donuts in one hand and a tray of drinks and hors d'oeuvres in the other. We are expected to smile and show grace and understanding as we perform before the audience. To do so skillfully, we need to stay focused and not lose our grip while hateful comments, slings, and arrows are aimed in our direction.

We have our own personal challenges of added weight to bring to the beam. These challenges can include family, work, and health issues. They can open us to anxiety, fear, despair, and other gremlins, in this case *aka* police-wives' "pitfalls" that take ahold. This extra load can keep us from performing our routines with ease.

The public, who fill the stands, have what Stacey Jernigan, a Dallas police wife, judge, and author calls "public misperceptions." She told me, "There are members of the public who absolutely hate our husbands. They think cops are all power-wielding, arrogant, hotheads." When they wave their signs of hatred, Stacey says, "You, as a LEOW may want to go out in the public squares and defend your spouse and his colleagues with a megaphone."

Jay says, "Police are seen under a microscope more than any other profession. You don't see doctors out on the streets performing operations, saving or losing lives. You don't see soldiers at war, judges deciding sentences, and lawyers prosecuting or defending. But society does see your husband—the police officer on the street, in the news, social media, and in the headlines daily."

So what happens when local or national reporters accuse or judge police officers before all the facts have been disclosed just to have a better storyline? Everyone watching or listening gets a skewed vision of truth, what Stacey calls pubic misperception. She adds the following:

> Critics who judge from the sidelines have no idea what it means to *live in the moment* and have to make a split-second decision. Our husbands cannot go and deliberate on things like politicians, judges, or business executives. They don't have time to call a meeting to get group input. They don't have think tanks, boards of directors, and consultants waiting in the wings when trouble breaks out. They have to make the tough calls, every day.

Over time, these negative comments give some people the "green light," so to speak, to be hateful. They overlook that police officers don't create the laws but work to restore order by enforcing the laws.

Of course, we really aren't performing acrobatic routines on a LEOW balance beam, but sometimes it sure feels like it. We are tugged and pulled from all sides, and our performances can be difficult and tiring. If we aren't careful, our feelings get hurt, and we become bruised all over from losing our grip and falling off our balance beam time and time again.

Unfortunately, a large number of LEOWs aren't able to keep their balance and perform successfully. They struggle and grow weary trying to avoid the slings and arrows of spectators. Some give up because the balance routine is just too complicated and the arrows that pierce their hearts go too deep. Some leave their husbands and the law enforcement world behind.

For those of us with the necessary strength, every time we get back on the beam it is with more determination and power than before.

Debriefing

Let's face it. Rejection and negativity from society can be painful, and it can affect our self-esteem. We need an extra layer of protection to keep the slings and arrows of the public from penetrating our imaginary bulletproof vest.

Keeping a healthy balance between our law enforcement lifestyle and the rest of society is challenging. Hatred from some members of society and sometimes, family members can make us angry, and open a window to a lot of emotional and health issues, especially fear and stress. Sometimes we feel the need to isolate ourselves, hoping to be shielded from what causes us pain. Where is the balance?

Bullet Points

Here are some preparation and performance tips to help you stay strong, confident, and balanced.

- Lead by example. Do not allow hateful actions of others to cause reciprocal actions that bring you down to their level. Instead, keep your distance and act with honor and dignity.
- Control your thoughts and actions. We have no control over what others say or do, but we can control our responses. Courage for a LEOW includes doing what is right despite harsh words from others.
- Keep the faith, stay proud and strong. My mom loved to tell me, "Sticks and stones can break your bones, but words will never harm you." Easy to say, but sometimes it is difficult to "turn the other cheek" and not allow the awful, hurtful comments of others to penetrate your heart.
- Evil and hate are out there, but love conquers all. Place your trust in the truth. First Corinthians 13:6–7 says, "Love does not delight in evil but rejoices with the truth. It always protects, always trusts, always hopes, always perseveres."

- Guard yourself from media overexposure. From time to time, you might need to limit yourself from reading and watching the news. I learned early in my journey as a police officer's wife to turn off the news and not let the negative attitudes of others bring me down. I felt the best way for me to keep from feeling angry was to not allow hateful, hurtful storylines to get inside my mind.
- Limit your social media times and the sites you follow. It's not possible to totally insulate yourself, so expect to experience a few friends' social media posts that are insensitive to your feelings—sometimes innocent, other times intentional.
- Be a voice that helps connect our two worlds together. Our responsibility, or duty if we choose it, is to help bridge the gap between law enforcement and society. If you join in a grassroots, organic effort to have your voice heard, do so with humility, grace, understanding, and a smile.
- I believe the more often society sees the "human" side of our LEOs, the more likely it can help build this bridge.
- Consider meeting your husband for lunch or dinner in public places.

Ephesians 6:16 says, "In addition to all this, take up the shield of faith, with which you can extinguish all the flaming arrows of the evil one."

BOLO 13

The Spice (aka Vice) of Life

Be on the lookout for an alias living in your home, one who resembles your husband, but poses as someone else. Something is very familiar about this man, yet something is drastically different. This man's appearance is slightly rough around the edges, which is a definite contrast to the clean-cut, straight-laced police officer you have grown accustomed to seeing at home. This alias also has started hanging out at the most unusual places in town.

J AY'S DUTY AS A homicide detective ended in 1988 when he was promoted to the rank of sergeant. In no time, he became well-known throughout the department as Sgt. Gus. His first supervisory duty was in the patrol division. However, it wasn't long before he was transferred back into the Criminal Investigation Division (CID), this time as the sergeant for the burglary unit. His time in CID as the burglary sergeant was short-lived because a new era of sexually oriented businesses began to appear.

The city of Arlington was growing by leaps and bounds. The APD felt it was time to separate the current narcotics unit in Special Investigation Division (SID) into two units, one for narcotics and the other for vice (immoral and illegal behavior). This separation created a new supervisory position in SID, and Sgt. Gus was chosen to be the first to take on the challenge of leading the newly created vice unit. He was thrilled. Three detectives were assigned to work with him.

A few weeks into his new position, Jay arrived home beaming from ear to ear. He proudly pulled an ID from his wallet, took a quick glance at it, and handed it to me.

"Well, what do you think?" he said with a smirk and a mischievous grin.

I took a quick look at the scruffy-looking man in the picture on the ID and then, just to watch Jay fidget, I slowly and methodically examined his new Texas driver's license. As I began to read out loud all the information printed, he began thumping the table with his fingers. The impatient jitter quickly led to an abrupt interruption.

"It's official. I now have an alias," he said, using his "anxious" voice.

"Well", I said kiddingly, "this ID says the man whose picture looks somewhat like you lives at a different address in another town, so I guess you need to start packing!" We both laughed, and then I said, "How cool. I'm excited for you, honey."

Closing my eyes ever so briefly, I thought, *Oh dear, here we go again. Another new adventure. I wonder where this roller-coaster ride will take us.*

Jay and I located an old, worn-out wallet in a drawer that would display his new ID through a plastic window. In the slot above it, he placed his new department issued credit card, also with his alias name. With a new sense of pride, he put the wallet into the back-right pocket of his slightly worn out jeans.

This assignment would require him to leave everything official about him at home while he was on duty. I watched as he stored his police badge and ID and patrol issued firearm. His personal wallet with his ID, business cards, personal pictures, and credit cards were placed in his lock box for safekeeping. Most importantly, he stored his wedding ring. It was official. He would no longer be Jay or Sgt. Gus when he was working.

His new position required him to look and dress like "nobody and everybody" except, of course, for his newly issued SID firearm, which, to this day I have no idea where he carried it. When I asked him, he said, "Well, it depends on what kind of case I'm working."

A *very ambiguous answer*, I thought to myself. He also needed to blend in, look normal, and be just an ordinary guy. Oh, and by the way, that "ordinary guy" had to like hanging out in bars.

It didn't take long for Jay to grow a scruffy-looking beard and hair that was just long enough to barely touch his shoulders. In keeping with the blend-in look, he made sure his hair, mustache, and beard were somewhat mismanaged. His alias profile was complete.

It seemed to be easy for Jay to conjure up this new identity, and I must say, he played the part very well. My new assignment, not as easy, was to see beneath all his scruffiness and get used to this changed man in my house and bed. Over the next two and a half years of our life, the conversations we had about his unusual work activities became, in my opinion, as bizarre as the alias name on his new ID.

The old Corvette with a horrible paint job and the beat-up truck he drove alternately in his new role were a far cry from the latest model of his unmarked take-home car that sat in our driveway while he was a detective in the CAPERS unit. These vehicles had been confiscated by the APD from arrested drug dealers and other criminals. His favorite to drive was, of course, the old Corvette. I wondered what our neighbors thought when Jay arrived home in that beat-up truck or old Corvette between the hours of two o'clock and four o'clock in the morning.

Jay (or I should say this alias) worked Tuesday through Saturday. He had Sunday and Monday off because, if you think about it, most people who choose a "vice-oriented" lifestyle are most likely to be sleeping off the long weekend binge on Sunday and Monday.

What exactly is a vice-oriented lifestyle? Evil, depraved, corrupt, and sinful are just a few of the words that might be used to describe the people my husband and his three detectives were working among. His new "beat" included every dive bar, strip joint, and massage parlor in Arlington. Prostitution, gambling, and alcohol violations were the top three vice crimes he talked about most often with me.

I learned quickly that being married to a vice sergeant was not for the faint or weak. Jay told me stories I wouldn't tell my best friend or even consider putting into this book. Shock factor topics became common, almost daily conversations that I never imagined I'd have with anyone. Blushing at every story got old. I decided to concede, suck it up, take a deep breath, and go with the flow. I realized his assignment was going to be "one wild roller-coaster ride."

Before Arlington's new totally nude strip club opened, Sgt. Gus and city officials worked steadily for months to finalize the new Sexually Oriented Business (SOB) section of the adult entertainment city ordinance. His expertise in law enforcement was helpful to the officials, who were attempting to take the crime (not fun) out of sex. They certainly didn't want their city to become a modern-day version of Pottersville, the fictitious town overflowing with burlesque shows, bars, and nightclubs in the classic movie *It's a Wonderful Life*.

Less than three months after the SOB section was finished and the ordinance was filed, the first totally nude establishment opened. Sgt. Gus's alias scheduled a meeting with the managers and employees to discuss the new SOB laws. In preparation, he enlisted me to help pick out a few unique items to add to his typical jeans and simple shirt uniform to conceal his identity from them. We found a full-faced ski mask and dark sunglasses. To look somewhat official, he decided to use his police windbreaker that had been stored in his closet. When he felt he had the look just right, he put everything on and modeled for me.

I thought to myself, *What a bizarre outfit!* Out loud I said, "I hope your meeting with the managers and strippers goes well."

When we both started laughing, I shook my head and said, "I can't believe I just said that!"

"I appreciate your support, dear," he replied sarcastically. He then took off the ski mask, sunglasses, and jacket to give me a kiss before heading out the door.

Wow, how strange. I thought, *what an interesting life we are living these days.*

I watched him drive away in the beat-up truck as he headed to the police station to check in and meet up with an officer who would drive him to the meeting. Together they rode in a patrol car to meet with the managers and employees. He wanted to make sure they knew and completely understood all the new ordinances. He also wanted to let everyone know that he and his detectives would be watching the employees' every move.

Jay called me after the meeting. "It went well, and I accomplished my mission." Then jokingly he added, "Well, of course most of the employees were fully clothed."

His sly remark wasn't worth responding to, so I just chuckled and said, "Stay safe, honey. I'll see you around four o'clock in the morning. Love you. Bye."

After he hung up, I shook my head back and forth and thought to myself, *Oh—my—goodness! Deep breath, Vicki. Just breathe and (hopefully) I will get used to it.*

This new strip joint (and the others that followed) soon became a hot spot for underage employment, alcohol violations, and other sexually oriented law violations. As a result, it kept Sgt. Gus's alias, and his detectives very busy.

One night he came home all excited and told me, in somewhat explicit detail, about an arrest of a visiting popular porn star from California he and his detectives had made. As Jay chuckled through his comment, he said, "I guess this porn star didn't read the fine print in the Arlington SOB section of the adult entertainment city ordinances before she took her act too far in one of her performances."

Oh brother, I thought to myself.

It wasn't long before this very busy vice unit was making the headlines. Some of the headlines were quite humorous. On September 26, 1991, columnist for the *Arlington Citizen's Journal* and professor at UTA (University of Texas at Arlington) Allan Saxe wrote, "I know what I want to be when I grow up. I want to be a vice officer. I wonder how somebody trains to be a vice officer?"

He continued sharing his thoughts on how to train for this job before he said, "According to the news reports, undercover vice officers viewed the woman dancing, considered it lewd, and called patrol officers to the club to take her to jail. Now I know that some jobs are tough. And being assigned to watch dancers undress is about the most demanding job I can imagine. But someone has to do it."

Sgt. Gus's alias and his team of detectives also organized prostitution stings to keep the streets of Arlington from becoming crowded with "girls of the night" and men, *aka* "johns," who were looking for "a date." The team even recruited a few female Arlington police officers to dress and walk the streets, all the while being guarded and recorded. Jay would say often, "The warmer the evenings, the higher number of johns arrested."

On July 25, 1993, a *Star Telegram* article stated, "Arlington police arrested fifteen men as part of a seven-month prostitution investigation on the west side. They were charged with prostitution and indecent exposure." Sgt. Gustafson was quoted as saying, "The men allegedly exposed themselves and/or offered or agreed to engage in sex for a fee with undercover officers."

The vice detectives also frequented certain massage parlors that were clearly not for the pleasure of a massage. According to the headline in the *Fort Worth Star Telegram* on October 20, 1993, "Adult tanning salons raided; two managers, five workers arrested." I laughed later when the Lifetime Movie *The Client List* came out in 2010. The tagline for the movie said, "A woman unknowingly takes a job at a massage parlor where prostitution runs rampant." Of course in the movie, just as in real life, the police raided the parlor and arrested the prostitutes and johns.

A wide variety of other activities kept Sgt. Gus's alias and his detectives busy, including sting operations, illegal gambling, high school underage drinking, and other alcohol and cigarette sales violations.

One of his detectives arrested a man for making a contract with him (the detective) to kill someone. *Seriously!* I clearly thought such activities were just Hollywood drama.

I'll never forget the day when Jay called me from work and said, "Oh my gosh, the perverts I arrested yesterday at the city park for indecent exposure and public lewdness are back again today!"

It must be frustrating for police officers to make arrests one day and within twenty-four hours, the offenders are back out on the streets, attempting to commit the same crimes. Needless to say, my family members and I were not allowed to frequent this particular park without being escorted by our own personal armed guard, my husband.

As Jay and his team worked their way through the bad and the ugly parts of our city, I was at the home front attempting to balance his life with the good and the beautiful. A warm welcome home with a genuine, happy-to-see-you smile would help brighten his day. Good, normal-life conversations would remind him how much he is loved and needed in our world.

With all that said, I had one steadfast rule for the days when Jay arrived home from this filthy, dirty, nasty job: "Honey, take a shower before you come to bed!"

I recall one benefit from his years in the vice unit. Jay loved continuing education. One of many documented hours of training through his twenty-six years on the police force was a gambling seminar he attended at Caesar's Palace in Las Vegas. I decided to go with him.

While he was in class learning all about the gambling industry, I was gambling with Caesar. My trip, of course, was on my dime; and a few dimes is about the most I won. Overall it was a fun trip, one in which we had a few moments of normal. A picture taken of us at dinner one night is still lovingly displayed on our bedroom dresser.

Sarah Williams, another police officer's wife, shared with me about her husband being undercover for eight years in the Irving Police Department and also working with Homeland Security. I asked Sarah what her biggest challenge is in being married to someone whose job is so demanding of his time and energy.

"Our biggest hurdle is working around his schedule. He works late evenings and is also on call. When he works through the night, he's tired the next day. With our four boys all close in age, that becomes a challenge. His unpredictable schedule makes it difficult for him to help with the boy's activities, which leaves most of the responsibility in my hands."

Despite these challenges, Sarah could see the good in their life, "He's a wonderful dad! He loves coming home to spend time as a family. Even though he has a demanding job and a difficult schedule, we all know it's an honorable job. He leaves his work at the door and does his best not to let it affect our home life. He's good at what he does, and the boys and I are very proud of him."

Sarah and I talked about some of the legal responsibilities police officers have working undercover. She told me how difficult it was for her husband to deal with the child pornography cases, as it would be for most officers. We agreed that our hearts and prayers go out to these children and the officers who work these cases.

On the lighter side, I shared with her about my one rule I had for Jay before coming to bed: take a shower! She laughed.

"So true! Every once in a while, Grant would arrive home and before anyone could greet him, he would say, 'Don't touch me! The place I worked today was full of filth, so I'm headed straight to the shower!'"

At the end of the interview, I asked, "Sarah, in general, what words of wisdom can you share?"

"Keep the faith," she said graciously. "Don't let fear be a part of your day. It can lead to anxiety. Nobody is truly in control of his or her time here on earth. Worry is a waste of energy."

Words of wisdom: We all need to keep the faith and keep the villain in God's hands.

Debriefing

As Jay and I traveled through this and many other phases and stages of his law enforcement career, I learned the importance of developing and improving my coping skills. I discovered I needed to wear not only my imaginary bulletproof vest to protect my heart and mind but also "the full armor of God," which is described in Ephesians 6:10–18. In fact, these coping skills were essential at one time or another through every position Jay held over the many years in police work.

Especially during those years of his vice work, it was necessary to keep communicating with Jay so I could support him and, more importantly, find the balance between the bad and the ugly with the good and the beautiful. With that said, too much information and not enough information were communication issues we continued to have. The more I knew, the more I didn't want to know.

So what do I want you to know if your husband works undercover? The number one word that keeps coming to the surface is TRUST.

Bullet Points

Here are some suggestions to help you deepen your thoughts.

- Trust your husband, and trust yourself.
- Trust your relationship. Have faith that your marriage is strong enough to ride this roller coaster.
- Trust his ability to do his job and do it safely. As Sarah said, "My husband knows how to take the precautionary measures to stay safe."
- Trust and understand that he has a job to do. He's not going to bars and adult entertainment establishments for pleasure.
- Trust in your ability and his desire to keep the lines of communication open. Especially trust his answer without further questions when you ask, "How was your night,

honey?" and his reply is, "You really don't want to know."
He's more than likely right; you really don't want or need to
know all the not-so-nice (vice) details. It's his job, not yours.

- Trust in your strength to be able to balance his life and yours
outside of his work with the good and beautiful, because he's
up close and personal with the bad and ugly at work.
- Trust Sarah's wisdom: "Work-life balance is so important. We
enjoy getting together with friends, and that helps to keep our
life in balance."

What else do I recommend? Just a few more "bullet points" to
add to the list.

- Read the Bible and stay connected with God. This simple act
will help him and you stay balanced.
- Attend church. Being around good and beautiful people is
always encouraging. Jay was off on Sunday and usually awake
in time to join us at the eleven o'clock service. If your husband
is working covert and feels he needs to limit his time in
public, find services you can watch together online.
- Watch for the gremlins to surface. Loneliness, isolation,
drugs, and alcoholism are a few to be aware of.
- Appreciate the great news. With this assignment, your
husband can stop at the store and pick up a loaf of bread
because he looks like "nobody and everybody."
- Remind yourself that "this too shall pass." Assignments such
as vice that require having an alias have a time limit. Many
police departments won't keep officers in covert positions
indefinitely. Thank goodness!

Ephesians 6:10–11 says: " Finally, be strong in the Lord and in
his mighty power. Put on the full armor of God, so that you can take
your stand against the devil's schemes.

BOLO 14

Unsolved, Unsettled

Be on the lookout for some cold days ahead. There seems to be that one mysterious case, which lingers and haunts a detective. It can follow him for a very long time. It is one that cannot be solved in an eight-hour workday. It may take a lifetime of analyzing.

I CAN'T PINPOINT THE EXACT day when Patsy Wright became a household name in our home. Over time, it just happened, and Jay entered that period of time in his detective life when an unsolved case began to haunt him. The Patsy Wright murder mystery is that "one case" where Jay found himself having to sit up at night, on and off, for over thirty years, wondering what he could have done differently and what it would take to solve the mystery.

This case is fascinating to many people, including me. It has all the components necessary to make headlines, and it certainly did at the beginning. It involves a beautiful woman in her early forties who died a mysterious death and was cremated before the toxicology report came back. And her home was wiped clean of any possible evidence that might have been left behind.

A tangled web of family finger pointing, lovers, ex-lovers, two ex-husbands, and a horse trainer took Jay, *aka* Detective Gus, to different parts of the state and into some unusual interviews. During the interview process of this case, Detective Gus also became aware of inconsistencies involving a large sum of money for the purchase of land in a small town just southwest of Fort Worth. Sadly, none of the widespread, evidence-chasing clues would bring the person who killed Patsy Wright to justice.

It all started one Monday morning in mid-October 1987. Before Jay could even get settled and begin his morning work routine, the CAPERS (Crimes Against Persons) sergeant walked in his office and dropped a death investigation report on his desk. She said, "Gus, something's not right here." His sergeant was right; something was very wrong.

Jay sat his coffee mug on the desk, removed his blazer, and rested it across the back of his chair. That move exposed his shoulder gun holster and his police badge, which was clipped to his belt and displayed his newly acquired, oversized, saucer shaped, award winning shiny belt buckle engraved with "Second Place 1987 Two-Man Calf Tie." In those days, Detective Gus resembled an old-school Texas style investigator, complete with the pearl studded snaps on his western cut shirt and well-worn cowboy boots. He reminded me of Chuck Norris in the popular *Walker, Texas Ranger* television show (excluding the cowboy hat).

As Jay read through the report, he shook his head in disbelief, thinking, *That's it? The officer collected a travel size bottle of NyQuil and nothing more? No crime scene investigator, no supervisor, no detective was called out?*

As he began to dig deeper into the report, he noticed the officer treated it as a routine injured person report—nothing more, and nothing less. The injured person, however, was a forty-three-year-old healthy woman who was pronounced dead at 4:15 a.m. shortly after arriving at the local hospital. Her body was then transported to the Tarrant County Medical Examiner's office for an autopsy. That moment was when Jay began his investigation into the mysterious death of Patsy Wright and the lifelong question, "Who dunnit?" Detective Gus contacted the medical examiner's office to find out how long it would take to get their findings.

"Homicide detectives are the ones who think *homicide* on all *death investigations* until they can prove otherwise," he once told me.

Eight long days later, he received a call from the medical examiner's office. "Are you sitting down?" said the voice on the other end of the line. "I haven't seen anything like this in over twenty years!" She then related that a toxicology test had revealed that Patsy Wright had died from strychnine poisoning. After a postmortem profile of the victim was completed, the medical examiner and Detective Gus agreed that the cause of death was *homicide*.

Detective Gus next retrieved from the evidence room the only evidence taken from her home, which was a six-ounce bottle of NyQuil. He had the remaining liquid tested. The results were astounding! There was enough technical pure grade strychnine in her travel bottle to kill seven to ten people.

This potent poison, known as the "lover's poison," is difficult to come by, especially in its purest form. Only about one hundred companies in the U.S. at that time used or sold pure strychnine. After ruling out product tampering and digging deeper and deeper into the interesting life of the victim, Detective Gus began to put together an investigation aimed at showing that someone close to Patsy killed her.

"She was targeted specifically, and the killer was patient and could bide his time," he told me. "It was well-known in the victim's circle of friends and family that she took NyQuil on a regular basis as a sleeping aid. When someone can go to the extent of putting a scheme together like this, there is no sense of urgency. The murderer knew that sooner or later she would take a dose of the poisoned NyQuil."

Detective Gus worked closely with the Tarrant County Medical Examiner's office, FBI, EPA, the Dallas Police Department's

Intelligence Division, and the Vicks Corporation. He also worked side by side with the polygraph examiner who performed polygraphs on "persons of interest" in this case. As Detective Gus continued to dig deeper into the entangled lives of those closest to her, he found interesting facts about each one that drew suspicion toward them.

Meanwhile the family hired a private investigator to try and solve the case. Jay must have thought this investigator had a big ego and just got in the way of his investigation, but he certainly understood the family reaching out to try and find answers and closure in whatever ways they could.

Patsy Wright was part owner of a wax museum. It so happened that a few years earlier, the receptionist also died a mysterious death. During the Pasty Wright investigation, Detective Gus was present when that receptionist's body was exhumed with the hope of finding a matching link of evidence to help solve the Patsy Wright murder mystery. No such luck.

D Magazine ran a story entitled, "Patsy Wright, Wax Museum Murder Mystery" in which Detective Gus was quoted: "Money is a good motive, and so is revenge, love, and hate. Sometimes it's just anger or retaliation. But who stands to gain by her demise? Who stands to lose if she doesn't die?"

Unsolved Mysteries, the popular TV show, brought representatives to town and interviewed Detective Gus for an episode about Patsy Wright's Murder Mystery. I had the pleasure of meeting the crew for dinner after they finished filming. It was pretty neat to meet everyone, but we didn't get to meet Robert Stack, the show's host at that time.

Once the episode aired, our friends and family members from all around called us and asked about the case. I only knew as much as Jay could tell me, but it was enough to carry on engaging conversations. The show's reruns ran for years. Of course, the police department and the show also would get calls from all sorts of characters with ideas and possible leads but no real answers.

Jay is the kind of person that must have all his t's crossed and i's dotted or he is left unsettled, so he became obsessed with the case. I'm sure his is the perfect personality for someone in this line of work;

however, all he could obtain was more circumstantial evidence. No hard evidence to make an arrest. He also had other cases on his desk that he was duty bound to solve.

To add stress to our daily lives, Jay decided it was time for him to prepare and take the Sergeant's Exam. His diligent studying paid off by being promoted to Sergeant Gus, which put him back on patrol at the supervisor level.

After he was promoted, the only case Jay handed over to the next homicide detective, unsolved, was the murder of Patsy Wright. To this day, the homicide is unsolved, which means Jay is still unsettled. From time to time, I hear disappointment in his voice whenever he talks about Patsy Wright's murder.

The thirty-year anniversary of this woman's death came and went. For Jay, it was a reminder of his years of disappointment and regret over not solving the case. Wonder and mystery still linger like a musty taste and scent that only time can bring, like an old attic filled with history, cobwebs, and dust particles that float in the air.

Debriefing

Your husband might have a case or two or a call that follows him, regardless of where he is in his career and even into retirement. This particular case was intriguing indeed, and Jay was deeply involved in it for a long time. He would spend his free time pondering and planning his next step, all with the hope of making an arrest. Eventually the lack of hard evidence bothered him to the point that he began to question himself and his theories.

Jay blamed himself for not being able to make an arrest and bring the murderer to justice. Days turned into weeks, which turned into months and years. Jay eventually moved on in his career but the case followed him emotionally.

As for me, I learned to express empathy. I listened as he revisited his steps and pondered what he might have done differently, especially later with updated technology.

Bullet Points

Here are some suggestions on how you can support your husband through tough times of disappointment and regret.

- Understand how an unsolved case or a call that didn't end the way he expected or hoped for can gnaw at him, causing disappointment to settle in.
- Disappointment is personal and can be difficult for some people to handle. Over time it can eat at their core. If your LEO doesn't get a handle on it, disappointment can turn into depression—something to watch for.
- If you see him going down the path to depression and the gremlin begins to take ahold of him, seek professional help—a counselor from the department, a Christian therapist, visits with friends and family whom you trust, possibly a coworker who has experienced this type of disappointment in his or her career can help.
- Life is full of disappointments, so it's important to support him and help him reframe his thought process. It can help move disappointment to a better perspective, which is a valuable lesson when other disappointments come.
- Let him have his space to ponder on the case. If he doesn't let his time thinking about it get to an unhealthy level, he should be fine.
- Let him know he's not alone. It is not uncommon for detectives to dwell on the what-ifs. Many "cold cases" are eventually solved because someone else takes on the case later.

- Listen to his concerns. Remind him how he did everything possible. Hopefully in his lifetime, someone may come forward or say something, which could solve the case.
- Remind yourself and him that someday someone will have to answer to God.
- Continue to pray and have hope. Jay and I pray that someday Patsy's killer will face the final judgment.

This Bible verse is comforting: "But they will have to give account to him who is ready to judge the living and the dead" (1 Peter 4:5).

BOLO 15

Communication Complexities

Be on the lookout for one of the biggest challenges: communication. Numerous books have been written about this subject, and experts offer seminars and weekend retreats to help couples communicate better. Very helpful indeed; however, law enforcement couples deal with additional communication complexities.

WHEN JAY AND I attended the nonmandatory but highly recommended meeting for police spouses, we heard the warning loud and clear, on how communication was vital to the success of a LEO marriage. We both took the advice offered seriously. That meeting had happened not long after he joined the force and was assigned to his Field Training Officer (FTO). To this day, we believe it helped us understand each other and allowed us the freedom to make important communication adjustments along the way: the good, the bad, and the ugly ones.

It isn't easy for any wife to communicate with her spouse, regardless of what he does for a living. Men and women think and communicate differently; they have different thought processes and different verbal and nonverbal communication styles. With the added LEO communication complexities in a relationship, communication can become messy.

I started noticing, after about a decade of Jay being in law enforcement, that on occasions he would bring his authoritative attitude and commanding voice home. As you can imagine, this way of communicating was not perceived as loving, warm, and fuzzy; especially when he was standing in front of me or the kids in uniform.

Somehow he had received my cheerful greeting, "Hi, honey, how was your day?" But instead receiving a similar, pleasant greeting, I'd get a quick response back, in a police-like demanding tone. No hello. Just a sharp, "Wait. I'll be with *you* a minute."

I'd bark back to him in a not-so-cheerful way. "Excuse me? I'm not one of the scumbags you have been dealing with, so back-off, dude!"

Yes, we were communicating, and yes, it was face-to-face, but it was just not in a healthy way. We agreed that Jay's tone was not acceptable and neither was my response. We made an effort to work together for a solution to this LEO communication complexity. Recognizing the gremlin (authoritative attitude) that had surfaced to cause the communication problem helped a lot.

His unfriendly responses, I learned over time, were usually because he was irritated about something that had happened at work. Sure, anyone can arrive home from work frustrated, and a short-tempered "response to a welcome" isn't pleasant. Nonetheless, when it comes from a police officer in uniform with an authoritative voice, it is perceived differently.

When I saw the signs of a bad day in his demeanor when he arrived home, I learned that he needed time to get out of his "command presence mindset" and "derig." The time he took to change his clothes helped him detach from the position of authority that comes with the uniform.

Law enforcement officers take classes on communication, supervision, and public speaking. They are taught how to use verbal and nonverbal communication skills for their work as well as recognize how others use them. But rarely do the same approaches work well at home.

When your officer comes home and uses his "job-training skills" of communication on you and the family, it can put a strain unintentionally on your relationship. At first Jay couldn't understand why the kids and I didn't like his command presence, authoritative voice, interrogation skills, or nonverbal communication as acceptable ways of communicating with us. Thankfully, like he did with his work clothes, he learned to "change out of" his work communication style when he came home (most of the time).

How can we as couples develop healthy communication at home that manages the complexities and challenges that are unique to LEO couples?

The foundation for all good communication is the skill of reading the communication style of each other. You can learn to pick up on your husband's style by observing the way he arrives home: *happy, quiet, sad, angry, agitated, non-responsive,* and so on. If his style is primarily verbal, you'll know that soon enough. If he prefers to communicate a lot with nonverbal signals, you'll have to learn to read them and draw him out into meaningful conversations.

After I came to know Jay's style and he mine, we could then discuss options on how to manage this communicational complexity. We worked together to help him leave his *work* communication skills at the door. I, in turn, learned to be more patient.

Retired APD Chief T. Bowman, PhD, shared a story that helped him and his wife deal with this challenge. "Shortly after I became Chief, we decided to get a new dog. My wife immediately named him Chief. When I asked her why, she said, 'Because there is only one chief in this house, and it's our dog!'" Now that was brilliant!

Another communication challenge law enforcement officers and their wives face is how to communicate while he is at work: how to use what I call "touch points," which means those quick check-ins by text or phone call. Especially in his line of work, touch points are important to us, if nothing else, for our peace of mind. However, our expectations of our LEO's touch points responses are sometimes not practical. His responses (or lack of) can be irritating or worrisome, which can cause the villain to surface.

Sergeant Travis Waybourn of the Mansfield Texas Police Department shared these words of wisdom.

> At first I didn't understand how important my communication would be for my wife, Cassidy. I had great communication with my officers, but I recognized that my wife and kids, who are the most important people in my life, weren't getting me at my best when it came to communication. Over time I learned her needs and began making special efforts to communicate better with her.

Cassidy's response brought the message home for me.

> We have been married for thirteen years now. And over the years, he's gotten so much better. He will take the time to send me a quick text or give me a call, if nothing else to say, "Can't talk. Okay." This simple but effective touch point keeps my worries and fears away. I'm proud to be a police wife.

I asked Caroline Gresham, the wife of APD Detective Michael Gresham, about how she and Michael communicate while he is on duty. She related the following:

> At first we texted. A lot. Sometimes he wouldn't or couldn't respond for hours, sometimes five or more. Sure it made me worry a bit, but I had to let it go and understand he was busy. I had to learn to accept this.

On average now, it's just a few touch points a shift or day.

When he was on patrol, I'd ask for his status. When he could, he would text a short response. As an example, he might text "DWI" (Driving While Intoxicated). This told me he was going to be working later than usual because it takes a long time to process a DWI incident. As wives of a law enforcement officer, we need to understand that when "duty calls," they respond. And if it's working overtime to finish a call or a case, we have to accept it.

Caroline warned about the consequences of unhealthy communication. "Unhealthy communication, for example, silence, resentment, distrust, and bitterness, can lead to unhealthy practices such as addictions or affairs. I don't feel it is in God's plan to have to exist in "my world" and not cross over to "his world." We must learn how to communicate and share our life with each other and find our level of comfort."

I believe the truth is that shift hours and part-time jobs can make it difficult to find the time to communicate. An officer is usually "all in" while on duty. Honestly, his communication with his family at home is not top priority during his shift, nor should it be. It is a communication complexity both of you will have to work through, all the while having faith in each other.

Caroline also shared how she has come to realize the importance of timely forgiveness, something all couples face, but it is distinctly different for LEO couples because officers literally put their lives on the line daily.

"I feel somewhat forced to find the place of peace out of necessity and fear that I might not see him again. I feel the need to finish with whatever the tiff was about before he goes back to work the next day. Sometimes we have to finish our dialogue via text. Thank God for modern technology in these cases."

Like Caroline, many times I too felt the need to find common ground after a tiff and before Jay went back to work the next day. In these instances, the surfacing of the villain was actually a helpful alert. The fear that our issue at that moment would forever be left unresolved helped me put our differences in perspective (most of the time). Usually whatever differences we were working through weren't worth him going to work the next day with the tiff hanging over both of us.

Another especially challenging LEO communication complexity may be his lack of interest in making decisions once he arrives home. Sometimes the demands of critical decision-making activities at work can cause officers to feel overloaded. Most have long work hours, and at times they are in a hypervigilant state of mind. When they finally arrive home, they may want to collapse and not have to make decisions. Some want to just sit in "the chair" at home, with no decisions to be made or demands to be met. Some might play mindless video games or stare at the television screen. In extreme cases, they may not want to communicate at all, be despondent and isolate themselves.

I used to wonder why Jay found it difficult to make decisions at home. Because of his job, most of the household decisions, including the discipline of the children, were on my shoulders. Still, there were times when his input was essential. Our house was super busy most of the time, so he didn't often have the luxury of coming home and sitting in "the chair" regardless of how he felt.

At first I didn't realize it was a job related issue. I thought it was a "guy thing." Looking back, it is clear to me now. Jay's personality is hyperfocused, sometimes intensely so, about what is important on his agenda at work.

When he came home from work, he would subconsciously "turn off" his hyperfocus, and leave the "nonhyper" decisions for someone else, meaning me. The good news was that he accepted my ideas and decisions (most of the time), rolled with the flow, and became active in decision making when I made it clear that his input was needed.

One of the biggest if not the biggest communication complexity for LEO couples is balancing "too much information" or "not enough information." My informational measuring bar of comfort—how much I needed to know—changed frequently. As a result, Jay had to adapt and adjust the amount of work-related information he shared at any given point in our relationship. The conversations or lack of conversations that took place were based on my ability to process them in a healthy way, what he thought I could handle, and his need to share.

From time to time I would get long periods of silence from Jay, which seemed to be his solution to my knee-jerk reactions to TMI. In response, my NEI would cause my creative imagination to work overtime. Finding the balance was so difficult!

I learned how certain assignments Jay held during his career challenged our TMI or NEI skills more than others. My comfort level moved up and down the scale more often when Jay was a homicide detective and a vice sergeant than when he worked in other assignments such as the School Resource Supervisor.

Here is an interesting story of TMI and NEI. I can tell you that it taught me a valuable lesson. Be careful what you ask for; you might not like what you get.

One Tuesday morning I was rushing out the door with the three kids in tow. Jay briefly and vaguely informed me that he would be adjusting his newly appointed, coveted, CID eight-to-five work hours and would be "working later than usual."

"Okay, do you know what time you will be home?" I asked.

"I don't know," he responded.

I didn't take the time to gather more details because I was already running behind to get the kids to school on time and then head to my job. Once I arrived at work, I didn't think much of our brief morning conversation. After all, my work was demanding and busy.

During this time in our life, I owned a wedding and catering business that was growing by leaps and bounds. Every Tuesday was our staff meeting. We discussed our past week's performances and upcoming receptions. Immediately after that meeting, I had back-to-back appointments with brides-to-be to discuss their plans, all with the hopes of securing more clients.

Jay called me around two o'clock in the afternoon to check in and remind me he would be working late. A brief "okay, love you and have a good day" was exchanged. At 3 p.m. as usual, I rushed out the door in time to be the last parent in line at carpool. The kids and I finished our after-school errands. When we arrived home, as expected Jay was gone.

Around 8 p.m., I slowed down enough to wonder *why* he was adjusting his work schedule for the day. After the kids were in bed, I kept myself busy with neglected household chores and the optimism of keeping the villain away. Shortly after 10 p.m., he called to say he was on his way home. When he walked in the door at last, I couldn't help but notice his plain-clothes uniform was adorned with a black windbreaker that said, "Arlington Police" on the back and he was carrying his bulletproof vest.

Hmm. Why is he wearing that? I thought to myself.

I asked him if he was hungry, and in an enthusiastic tone he said, "Starving, but no pizza!"

What a weird comment, I thought.

"Okay, good thing because we don't have any pizza," I replied.

He took off his jacket and set it down next to his vest, went to the sink, scrubbed his hands and arms thoroughly, and then scrubbed them one more time for good measure. While I was heating up his meal of leftover baked chicken and broccoli casserole, I asked him my famous question.

"So, honey, how was your day?"

With a wink and a smirk, he reached for me and gave me his extra special I-made-it-home kiss and bear hug. He then reached into the refrigerator, opened two beers, and handed me one.

I could see he wanted to tell me all about his work that night. In his previous assignments, we had worked through the TMI and NEI and reached a comfortable level in communicating. With this new assignment, we were in unchartered territory.

We sat at the table. I went first. I touched briefly on the kids and shared my excitement about the two brides who had secured their reception with me that day. My topics of conversation ended quickly with a smile and a "that's great, Vicki" comment from him.

Jay then finished scarfing down his meal. My guess was he hadn't eaten all day. Just as the last bite hit his stomach, his conversation began. He proceeded to tell me how he was able to make a successful felony arrest of a suspect that two days earlier had murdered someone. All of what he shared was brand-new information to me.

Jay, *aka* Homicide Detective Gus, related the story to me as if I were one of his police buddies—offering all the facts of this case, including the dangerous details. The suspect lived in a small, downstairs apartment on the east side of town. A few days prior to this night's arrest, APD had responded to an anonymous call about a male victim who was found dead in an unkempt flowerbed (which turned out to be right outside the suspect's apartment). Homicide Detective Gus was called to the scene. At that time, no witnesses were located, and the victim had no identification on him.

This particular felony arrest, Jay shared, required the SWAT team to make entry into the apartment where the murder suspect had resided.

I tried to hide my uneasiness as the story unfolded by playing with the almost empty beer can, but my loud and questionable blurt-out, "SWAT team?", was a dead giveaway.

He replied quickly, "Yes, dear. SWAT," and then continued the story. He told me how he created a profile to determine the victim's identity and later the suspect's identity.

"It was a long process getting to the arrest warrant," he said. "I had to figure out who the victim was. Then how the victim and suspect crossed paths. Find out who lived there, watch the apartment, make sure they still lived there, and develop enough probable cause for a judge to sign the warrant. All my i's had to be dotted and t's crossed before I, and yes, dear, the SWAT team, could go to work tonight."

Jay clearly was proud to have worked with his fellow officers. He went on to tell me how they knocked open the door forcefully (tactical style, of course), secured the apartment, and apprehended the suspect. As his story continued, my heart rate rose, and I rubbed my sweaty palms against each other. One by one, my legs began to bounce up and down and my breathing became deeper with each new development.

Stay calm, Vicki, I thought to myself. *He's fine and sitting right here! Quit squirming and breathe. Wow. TMI. The reality of finding and arresting murder suspects is uneasy for me and more dangerous for him than I anticipated it to be. I began to wonder how often I'd have to keep the villain away throughout this new assignment.*

Jay said there were two males and one female inside the apartment. He then made sure I understood specifically how the SWAT team secured the apartment, which included handcuffing all three who were inside.

Oh, okay, I get it, I thought to myself. *Knowing you went in <u>after</u> the SWAT team is supposed to worry me less? Sorry, dude. I don't think so. Just because everything went down like a textbook case this time doesn't assure me it will the next. Where are my cigarettes? Oh, that's right. Jay and I quit smoking a while back. Darn it.*

Jay continued without noticing the look on my face. *Major nonverbal communication missed.*

"I holstered my gun, identified myself to the suspect, and served the warrant. As we searched the apartment for evidence and weapons, one of the tactical team members said, 'Hey Gus, I guess we really surprised them when we made entry! Look at the pizza stuck to the ceiling.'"

Jay chuckled lightheartedly and said, "Everyone in the room looked up and saw what was left of the pizza. It was dangling from the ceiling."

"Oh, funny! That's why you didn't want pizza!" I said, doing my very best to digest his unnerving story.

He must have sensed my nervous reaction to "the case of the dangling pizza." After his rendition of the SWAT team's heroic entry and his arrest, the silence began. Weeks upon weeks went by with little to no communication. My "how was your day, honey" question received only his simple "fine, dear" answer. He'd then quickly redirect the conversation to anything but his work.

During that time, I was still getting used to his new position. Not enough information during our daily conversations was almost worse than TMI. The NEI allowed my very vivid imagination to appear in technicolor images. I began creating scenarios in my head. "The case of the dangling pizza" turned into "the case of a cop-murdering psychopath." The villain surfaced again and circled around in my mind like a buzzard ready to pounce. My normal worry turned into full-blown fear.

What is he _really_ *doing eight-to-ten hours a day?* I wondered. Eventually I would have to confess what was going on inside of me and ask him.

"Jay, you have clammed up," I said one day, "And not enough information is causing me more worries and concern than necessary. I know, you're thinking about my past responses to TMI, but please tell me now what your day is really like." With fingers crossed behind my back, I added, "I can handle it, really!"

Sugarcoating to protect me, he said, "Vicki, dear, it's just a lot of office work. In a nutshell, I read crimes against persons reports and then make calls and do interviews. Yes, sometimes I'm required to respond to a crime scene where there has been a death. Then I file a case, get a warrant, and eventually make arrests."

Relieved, I thanked him. He then promised he would do a better job of sharing his day with me.

Remember when I said earlier, "Be careful what you ask for. You might not like what you get." Well, the very next week, when Jay arrived home in the evening— after adjusting his 8-to-5 work schedule *again*—he found me chilling in bed and watching something lighthearted on the TV. He, on the other hand, was jumping at the chance to share his workday with me. He reminded me in that moment of our six-year-old son, anxiously ready to show me the latest bug he'd found in the yard.

I think I'm about to get TMI'd, I thought to myself.

His words were like a cloudburst, overflowing with information about a new case he'd been working. A woman had been strangled and beaten to death. The murderer had attempted to set her on fire to cover his crime. Jay's drought of silence had turned into a downpour of gory details. As he was attempting to explain the crime scene more vividly, he reached into his pocket and pulled out a picture.

"Here," he said. "This is what my week has been like!"

I gasped. The photo of this woman was gruesome and sad. Certainly not something most people would or should ever see.

Seriously? How nice of him to "TMI me" with an unofficial, show-and-tell photo of this poor, dead woman. And at bedtime, in my bed!

My immediate and next thought was, *He might be able to turn off this visual image and sleep like a baby, but I'll have nightmares for days of me being held captive in "The Towering Inferno."*

The image of an actual person whose life had been ended by evil hands would forever be etched in my mind. And to think, Jay was there, seeing and working the crime scene in person.

"Okay, Jay, thank you for sharing your week, but sorry, once again it is a little too much information for me. In the future, I'll happily take the sugar-coated version without the visual aids of real dead people, at least not at bedtime."

Our extreme communication efforts, from "too hot" (TMI) to "too cold" (NEI), were beginning to feel like a Goldilocks porridge story. At least on that we agreed. With that said, we would keep trying and would eventually find the "just right" amount of information to make us both happy.

As the years flew by, my ability to handle more information grew. I began to learn and understand more. Still, he and I both learned a valuable lesson: I can live my entire life without ever seeing a real crime scene or photos of them.

Yes, our LEO communication complexities can be challenging. Sometimes his authoritative tone, mixed with TMI or NEI can throw us off balance. However, with open communication and willingness to adjust and accept the good, the bad and the ugly we can have togetherness.

Debriefing

Although my measuring bar of comfort for hearing details about Jay's work is really high now, I still have my limits. After reading this chapter, you might come to the realization that your personal bar is exceedingly high. You can handle the gory details and want to know all of them. Or, on the other hand, you might be on the lower end of this bar.

Wherever you are, try not to get discouraged. Through healthy communication with your spouse, you will find the "just right" amount.

As you face this and other communication complexities, only some of them covered in this chapter, it is good to remind yourself that your LEO needs and wants good, healthy communication with you. He's learning as he goes along too.

Author and speaker Andy Stanley offers a study for couples called *iMarriage*. In this study, Stanley speaks freely about expectations in a marriage versus desires. He equips women and men with a way to put the focus on the spouse instead of the self. The results can be life changing.

Drs. Les and Leslie Parrott, a husband and wife author team, specialize in helping build (or rebuild) healthy couple relationships. In their book called *Love Talk* is a chapter titled, "Communication 101: Brushing Up on the Basics." In this chapter they share their thoughts and ideas on the basics in communication. A few of them stood out to me. One of them is called "Making Time for Talk." They say, "Time and talk are always a winning combination … If you want to improve your communication, you must ruthlessly eliminate hurry from your conversations."

The other basic skill in their book that stood out to me was called "Attending Skills." They say, " … attending. This is the word communication specialists use to describe the physical and psychological attention you give your partner during a conversation. These are the nonverbals that can make or break your connection."

In my opinion, law enforcement couples can't stop with just the basics. We can't dismiss the communication complexities that are unique to us. Understanding and coping with them can be a significant and ongoing challenge. And keep in mind they can open the door for the villain to enter.

Bullet Points

Here are some practical tips and ideas to ponder as you learn to navigate the unique communication complexities you both may be faced with.

- Consider reading this chapter together. Discuss the communication complexities the two of you are facing right now.
- "There are two parts to communicating: the sender and the receiver," Jay reminds me.
- Healthy relationships need face-to-face communication, often. It sounds so simple to say, "Talk to each other." But it is too easy to rely on other styles of communication that are less effective and leave room for misinterpretation. If you wonder why your relationship isn't working, find the time to have face-to-face, healthy conversations.
- Texting is not a substitute for face-to-face communication. You cannot see an expression, feel emotions, or hear tones through a text. Emojis are not real.
- Phone calls can't touch on all the senses needed to communicate in a healthy way.
- Although you can see the other person during Facetime, you can't smell or touch each other. Make your precious time together count.
- Law enforcement officers need someone willing to listen and understand. The idea that your spouse can leave all of his job stresses at work is unreasonable for most LEOs. I often

wonder, if the officer isn't talking to his spouse, to whom is he talking? Even worse, is he communicating at all?

- Talk to your husband about your personal measuring bar of comfort. Know and understand that it can change. Adjust as needed. Have faith that you will find the "just right" communication together. As Caroline said, "There is definitely a learning curve. It is an ongoing, constant conversation between us, and most of the challenge is based on his position at the time. My comfort level constantly changes."

- I personally recommend that you don't listen all day to a police scanner or follow the "active call" list online regularly while your husband is on duty. At first it can be fun and exciting, but it can become addicting and unhealthy. You could be adding more loops or sudden drops to an already stressful, roller-coaster life.

- Consider attending a retreat together.

- Look for retreats designed for law enforcement officer couples, which focus on addressing the unique emotional and spirituals needs law enforcement officers and their families face.

- Chris Kyle Frog Foundation offers retreats for military and first responders. *https://www.chriskylefrogfoundation.org/*

- Bless the Badge offers "Tactical Relationship Training", their trademark couple counseling and conference. The also offer workshops. *https://blessthebadge.org/*

- Blue Marriage offers an online twelve-month police marriage academy. *https://www.bluemarriage.com/*

- Most relationships have challenges, including those lasting fifty years or longer. If those relationships had an excellent record of ninety percent sunny and bright times together, they still experienced ten percent of dark and difficult times. Using this example, we can calculate that a good and lasting relationship includes forty-five sunny and bright years and five years of difficulty and darkness. So in your difficult times, remind yourself to keep the faith and trust that sunny and bright days will come again.

- Consider Chief Bowman's words: "A biblical marriage is surrounded by and connected by your faith. Practicing good communication skills, along with exercising the three great Christian virtues of faith, hope, and love, will help get you through the tough times."

- I believe faith and a lasting relationship go hand in hand. Faith is not visible or tangible; it is knowing you will get through, even when you can't see the way. You trust in God and his promises. "Keeping the faith" gives you somewhere to turn for answers when there aren't any. Without these Christian virtues of faith, hope, and love, I believe our marriage would have failed.

First Corinthians 13:13 says, "And now these three remain: faith, hope and love. But the greatest of these is love."

BOLO **16**

Sacrifices

Be on the lookout for sacrifices. You and your husband will sacrifice time away from each other and he from the children and family activities. Your husband might sacrifice his health because of the burdens he carries or the injuries he endures. Most law enforcement families eventually sacrifice their innocuous view of the world. The hardest sacrifice is to accept that some officers will make the ultimate sacrifice, their life.

I T IS NO SURPRISE that our husbands' job changes them. Their job also changes us, the wives. By extension, our families' lives change as well.

One of the most immediate changes is his overprotectiveness. It bleeds into our simple space, changing us along the way. It gives us, the wives, a burden of our own to carry as well—a heightened awareness of danger and evil, causing us to sacrifice the freedom of unconsciously feeling free from potential danger.

In contrast, friends and family outside of the police world can be oblivious to their surroundings and trustworthy of the world around them, without much thought that someone might cause harm to them. Because cops deal with the bad and ugly of our communities, the average person's lifestyle can feel free and unrestricted.

I'm a big fan of the popular TV show *Blue Bloods*. Here is part of what one of the characters said, in so many words, about this luxury in the episode aired on September 27, 2017: "There is something you should know about police officers. They know what people are capable of in a way that most, thankfully, do not ... They assume the worst, and they take that on so that good people can go about their lives and think generously about their fellow man. They provide that luxury."

Another sacrifice you might have already experienced is the challenge that police officers' schedules can be unpredictable. This is such an important topic for LEOWs, and I address it many times in this book. It is a sacrifice because, in contrast to the *Flintstones* cartoon show, officers don't get to go home like Fred does when the bird squawks. Instead, their work hours are as unique as their job.

They and you more than likely have experienced his job as a twenty-four-hour, seven-day-a-week, three-hundred-sixty-five-day-per-year position with no guaranteed time off for holidays. It is a job in which the words *mandatory* and *time off denied* are commonplace. Officers are on call even during their lunch breaks.

When they are working a late call, an urgent or complex case, or a special assignment, they sacrifice their time off by working the extra hours to complete their shift. Many officers also sacrifice their free time off the job by working part-time jobs so they can pay bills that pile up.

The result of the unpredictability of officers' schedules is less time for themselves and their families. This sacrifice is essential for you to understand *and accept*; otherwise, it can corrode your marriage.

It is also not uncommon for officers to struggle with health issues that may be a result of their job. As an example, some officers struggle with high blood pressure or battle alcoholism or depression.

Injuries from the job are another example of health sacrifices. Answering a call can become physically demanding in an instant. A criminal resisting arrest or an angry crowd can cause an injury. Anytime firearms or lethal weapons are involved, there is a potential for an intentional or even an accidental discharge. Even training exercises can cause injury or death. Some injuries are short-lived, while others are more serious and may last a lifetime.

The ultimate sacrifice, which has LEOWs fighting the villain of worry and fear all too often, is loss of life. According to the National Law Enforcement Officers Memorial Fund (NLEOMF), the death of an officer happens about every sixty hours in the United States. This statistic creates a somber effect on officers and their families.

I will never get used to how I feel when an officer dies in the line of duty, paying the ultimate price for service. So many emotions are triggered inside me. They usually start with disbelief and then immediately move to sadness. My heart begins to feel heavy, and the more I learn about the incident, more emotions begin to surface, including anger and frustration. My imaginary bulletproof vest sometimes cannot keep the pain from breaking my heart, especially when a loss of life happens within my husband's department.

Jay and I recall a tragic event that happened one summer evening, June 7, 2001, during a time when he was a patrol sergeant. That evening he was conducting a friendly neighborhood watch program for the citizens in his district. During the middle of his presentation, his police radio broadcasted "10–34" (officer down), which means one of his fellow officers was critically injured or killed.

"A broadcast like that one instantly has your heart skipping a beat," Jay said. "My entire demeanor changed; however, there was no request for additional officers, so I had to maintain my composure and finish my presentation. Afterward I went to my patrol car to wait for more information. I'm sure all the officers who were able to do so were doing the same thing. As I sat there, listening about one of my fellow officers who was killed, a wave of emotion poured over me. I was in disbelief, and I remembered feeling numb."

The signal code was broadcast around six-thirty in the evening, and Jay's shift didn't end until eleven. He called me around seven-thirty to let me know he was okay but one of our officers had been killed. He went on to say, "It's going to be a tough, long night, and I will give you more details when I get home. I love you."

I remember thinking, *How can this be? This poor family. I just can't imagine what they are going through right now.*

The villain began to surface inside my mind, and I fought to keep it away. *Just breath, Vicki. Jay is okay.*

After turning to God in prayer, I then turned on the news very briefly to gather more information. Over the next five hours, I mindlessly paced the floor, impatiently waiting for Jay to arrive home.

Around midnight Jay walked across the threshold of our home, his head and shoulders slightly slumped forward. He was clearly saddened and burdened by the tragic event that had taken place, as was I. It seemed surreal to us both. The black band memoriam was already wrapped around his badge. Seeing the band reminded me how real this news was. At that moment, Jay needed to share this story with me, and I needed to know the details myself so we could both begin to process this loss of life. The tears began to flow.

A tragedy such as this one is difficult to recover from on many fronts. "It can have an effect on the entire police department," said Jay. "My department offered counselors and peer support to the officers who were struggling to cope. The chaplain was also available for officers and their family members."

I recall Chaplain Elliott telling me, "Usually when an average person's family member dies, the world stops for those left behind. They drop everything and surround themselves with loved ones for comfort. When you are a police officer, however, the world doesn't stop because one of your own dies. Dispatchers continue to send out calls, and officers continue to answer those calls, knowing all the while that just a few miles away a friend, partner, and police family member was just killed. It's tough!"

On December 28, 2010, Arlington Police Officer Jillian Smith paid the ultimate sacrifice. She was dispatched to a domestic dispute, where she ultimately shielded an eleven-year-old child with her own body. This courageous act saved the young girl, but Jillian received a fatal gunshot wound.

She was a hero. Her selfless act of bravery exhibited her love and compassion for others. Every time I think of her bravery and sacrifice, I can't help but be reminded of this Scripture verse, John 15:13: "Greater love has no one than this: to lay down one's life for one's friends." Jillian selflessly and honorably laid down her life for this child.

On August 28, 2015, in broad daylight, Deputy Darren Goforth of the Harris County Sheriff's Department stopped at a gas station to fill up his patrol car. Someone ambushed him from the back, killing him instantly. He had been targeted simply because he was wearing a uniform. He was laid to rest as a hero who dedicated his life to his family and community. His ultimate sacrifice is one of the reasons *His Badge, My Story* was written (see the Introduction).

The July 2016 Dallas police officer massacre happened only a few miles away from where Jay and I live. This awful loss of life and their ultimate sacrifice affected their families and police communities across the country. Our country's Blue Nation began the grieving process together. Kind and caring citizens everywhere sent their love to Dallas.

The nature of this mass murder of police officers was tough to grasp. JoAnne, Police Officer Robert's wife, said, "It was difficult. I worried and feared for my husband. I worried for our local community. I wondered if more mass shootings of police officers would happen in the weeks that followed. Robert and I went to the funeral of Patrick Zamarripa. It was my first police officer funeral, and it has had a lasting effect on me."

It is unfortunate, but during your journey as a law enforcement officer's wife, you will experience many stories of the ultimate sacrifice. They will touch your heart and bring to the surface a web of emotions, including the villain of worry and fear you struggle with the most.

The next three stories are about amazing women who showed strength, courage, sacrifice, and hope. They are survivors.

Theresa's Story

Theresa Lozada is a remarkably strong woman. Meeting her, I instantly perceived she loves deeply. Theresa and her husband, Victor, knew each other from childhood. When they married, Theresa asked two things of him. One was never to become a police officer. Two was never to be a motor officer.

Seven years after they were married, she conceded. Together they agreed Victor could follow his lifelong dream of becoming a police officer and eventually a motor officer. He loved his job, and they embraced the world of law enforcement.

This couple learned to work through the challenges of shift schedules and family traditions by being creative. They figured out ways to spend time together as a couple and a family, despite his schedule. Theresa shared how they included Victor in each family tradition, regardless of what the clock said. As an example, to celebrate a child's birthday, he and Theresa would wake up the birthday child and the siblings at 4 a.m., just before Victor left for work. With a cupcake and candle in hand, they would sing the happy birthday song. Their kids loved this tradition.

Because dinner was an important time for them, they would meet often during Victor's dinner breaks. Yes, he was in uniform, but that didn't matter because they were living life together and creating memories.

On their wedding anniversary dates when he was working, they would find a way to spend some time together alone. Theresa treasures a special anniversary card Victor gave her on July 26, 2007. In it he wrote: "Let's make this time together count, as if it was the very last" (not realizing it would be their last).

Theresa was active in her police wives' community and spent time with other wives who understood the challenges. Christian relationships were important to both of them. Although Victor wasn't always able to attend church regularly, they raised their children in a church home.

On February 22, 2008, Senator Hillary Clinton came to Dallas. When someone important comes to town, motorcycle officers are assigned to escort the dignitary to and from the destinations. Victor was one of the motor officers on the escort team that day. He was very excited to perform this duty and considered it an honor. During the escort, while traveling over the Houston Street viaduct, Victor hit a cement barricade. His motorcycle slipped and crashed. His helmet flew off, and his unprotected head hit the cement. He died at the scene.

"Because of the political nature of his death," Theresa shared, "there was confusion and chaos, with little to no privacy. Officers were like angels to me and hovered over me until I calmed down. Because of the chaos, I couldn't get ahold of our children in time to share the news before they heard it from outside sources."

The relationships Theresa and Victor had developed in the police community and the larger community were a tremendous resource in the ensuing days and weeks. Officers and their families continued to be there. Her church friends surrounded her with support and comfort. Her immediate and extended family members were also there for her, and she leaned on them.

"Even to this day, she shared, the family gatherings continue." From time to time, she and her children meet at Victor's gravesite and feel at peace, with no regrets. This loving statement of hers still rings in my head: "They know they have a future because of the way he lived."

During the precious time I spent with Theresa, she said more than once, "I have no regrets, because our love has no boundaries." These words express how living the LEO life together as a couple and creating memories of love, laughter, and family traditions can last into the future, even a lifetime.

Maria's Story

I spent the first fall-like chilly morning of a recent October day having brunch and visiting with another survivor, Maria Barreda-Alvarado, who Theresa met after Victor died. Maria was a volunteer at that time for an organization called C.O.P.S. (Concerns Of Police Survivors). When Theresa reached out to C.O.P.S., Maria answered her call.

Maria and I were friends on Facebook, and I'd seen her at events that involved the law enforcement community for many years. Until our brunch time together that day, however, we didn't know each other personally, nor did I know her story. It didn't take me long to get to know this amazing woman who turned *her* tragic loss into compassion for others and has touched countless lives of men and women in law enforcement.

Maria shared her emotionally charged story of how her life changed on Valentine's Day 1997. Her son, Corporal Rick Barreda of the Dallas Fort Worth Airport DPS (Department of Public Safety), was killed in a motorcycle accident while in pursuit of a speeding motorist, leaving behind a wife and two daughters, parents, siblings, and many other loved ones.

For Maria, the loss of her son was devastating. She became withdrawn from family and friends, depressed, and desperately wanting to see her son again.

"You know how some people say there is a hole in their heart when they lose a child or loved one?" she shared. "Well, I feel mine deep in my gut. I think of him every day."

Through tears that were as fresh as those she shed that Valentine's Day years ago, she told how she found healing.

"I could have stayed stuck in the past with anger and bitterness. However, with love from my family members, volunteers with C.O.P.S., the power of the Holy Spirit, and my faith in Christ, I learned to live with the loss and grief that was so deep within me. I began to connect with others who were in the same situation, and this offered me hope. I learned that death might end a life, but not a relationship; we own that, because love never dies."

Maria's compassion for others ultimately led her to dedicate her life to helping the law enforcement community. Because the C.O.P.S. organization was there for her, she became involved with the local C.O.P.S. chapter and eventually became president. Her role as a comforter included offering her support in the worst of times.

"It was tough, but I found it vital to attend countless funerals over the fifteen years I was with C.O.P.S. Just showing up made a difference to others."

Wow, I thought to myself, *Maria discovered the strength inside her to be brave enough and become a light to others.*

Her story didn't end there. In 2012, she founded Peace Officers Angel Foundation (P.O.A.F.). Its mission is to offer emotional and short-term financial assistance to Texas law enforcement officers following a serious or life-changing injury. Maria travels throughout the Lone Star State, speaking and engaging with others to help with this cause.

During our time together, Maria shared these beautiful words: "Love and remembrance never falter in spite of the years." I will not forget them or her sacrifice.

When Maria and I were ending our brunch date, my heart filled with joy as she shared this closing statement: "I continue to hold onto the few words Ricky said to me the last time I saw him— 'I love you, Mom.'"

Jessica's Story

Through P.O.A.F., Maria reached out to Jessica Gass, a young police wife whose husband suffered a severe injury. Jessica is also a woman of strength, courage, and faith. Their story of sacrifice is an inspiration to me.

Jessica and her husband, Houston Gass, were married in July 2014. Their life together as a new, young, blended family was going smoothly until January 6, 2015. On that day, the department Houston worked for was shorthanded, so Sergeant Gass went in early and then straight to assist in a domestic dispute call. Meanwhile, Jessica had begun her day as usual by getting their three kids off to school and then going to her office.

Around 11:30 a.m., Jessica looked out the window and noticed two patrol cars pull up and stop right in front of her office. Her husband had been an officer for thirteen years, and she knew these officers.

Maybe they are just coming by to visit, she thought at first. But as they were walking in, she noticed their somber, serious looks of concern.

"Jessica, can we talk someplace private?" one of the officers said.

After the three moved to her boss's office, the unexpected words came. "Houston has been shot."

Her immediate response was, "Is he alive? Where was he shot? Was it serious?" Her mind and her words began to stumble over each other as she processed what she was hearing. Anxiety rose to the surface.

The officers shared, "All we know is that while answering a domestic dispute call, he was shot in the face with a shotgun, and he is being flown to Amarillo trauma center right now."

Based on their horrific description, neither Jessica nor the officers were sure Houston would survive. He'd been rushed by helicopter to the Amarillo trauma center. The officers made arrangements to have the grandmother pick the children up from school, and they drove Jessica in the patrol car to the hospital.

When they arrived at the hospital, the doctors were in full swing, working diligently to save his life and what was left of his left jaw. He was then transferred almost immediately to Lubbock University Medical Center. When he awoke, he had a tracheotomy, tubes, bandages, and a lot of swelling. He couldn't talk and had lost most of his teeth.

On Saturday, four days after the shooting, the kids were brought to see their daddy. Jessica remembers telling them, "Daddy got shot by a bad guy and has a big booboo. He can't talk right now because his face is bandaged up." The kids handled the visit well.

Ten days after the shooting, Houston was released to Jessica's care. Over the next days, weeks, and months, Jessica assisted with his home-health care and administered antibiotic shots and cared for his wounds. The healing process was slow, painful, and grueling. Houston and Jessica would travel back and forth to Lubbock and then eventually to Dallas for endless numbers of reconstructive surgeries.

"My anxiety would some days be extremely difficult. Grief and anxiety can make you breathless." Jessica said.

As she shared these challenges with me, she also said, "Sometimes it's good to give in so God can do his work."

At the time of this writing, Houston has gone through seventeen surgeries with more in his future. The shooter, a convicted felon, received fifty years with no chance of probation at thirty-five years.

The trauma, surgeries, and criminal trial put a strain on their marriage. Jessica said, "Without faith and support of family and friends, our marriage would have failed. Houston didn't want to put me through the long, painful experience. But my love and faith were unwavering."

Houston was unable to return to work for two years. Amazingly, he accepted a position as Chief of Police for Fritch, Texas, a small town not far from their home.

"Why go back?" I asked.

"It is a calling," Jessica shared. "He loves what he does and is great at it. If he were to die, it would be doing something he loves. I support him, respect and honor his desire to go back to work in law enforcement."

During one of their many trips to Dallas, Jay and I had the pleasure of meeting them for dinner. Houston was in town this time for another surgery on his jaw and teeth. His attitude, will, and faith were positive and strong. He told us he is helping other officers who were injured in the line of duty by listening to their stories and sharing his experience.

Because of his personal sacrifice and willingness to help others, Houston Gass was awarded the LET (Law Enforcement Today) Citizen of the Year 2017. Well deserved.

Debriefing

As you read through these sacrifices, you might have found yourself shaking your head in agreement with some and in disbelief with others. You also may wonder if you have what it takes to be strong enough to endure the piercing pain in your heart when you learn of a law enforcement officer who was seriously injured or lost his or her life in the line of duty.

You might experience a secret feeling of relief that it wasn't your husband. You might also experience guilt for privately thanking God it wasn't him. Eventually I hope you will experience a feeling of pride in knowing that your husband is in the same profession, travels the same roads, walks the same steps, and has the same servant heart as one who would sacrifice their own health or life to save others.

The "bullet points" for this chapter include suggestions and words of wisdom from Maria, Jessica, and Theresa. I encourage you to look back at the following BOLOs, especially the Debriefing sections, because they offer suggestions on how to handle the situations mentioned in this BOLO:

> BOLO 3: The Villain *aka* Worry and Fear
> BOLO 11: Gremlins *aka* Pitfalls
> BOLO 12: Balancing Act
> BOLO 15: Communication Complexities

Maria's, Jessica's, and Theresa's lives have been altered forever. I am so grateful for their willingness to share their stories and show us how to find hope and a way to cope with a serious injury or loss of life. If we find ourselves in a similar situation, we can hope to move forward with peace and no regrets. I believe these suggestions will help you find your inner strength as you continue your journey as a LEOW.

Bullet Points

Maria shared these words of wisdom for those who have lost a loved one in the line of duty:

- Death ends a life but not a relationship. You own that because love never dies. Love prevails over everything.
- It is important for parents to be able to stay in relationship with daughters-in-law or sons-in-law if a son or daughter is killed in the line of duty. Parents want desperately to be a part of their grandchildren's lives.
- Reach out to organizations that have the resources to help you through the tough times. The two mentioned in this chapter, P.O.A.F. and C.O.P.S., can be a starting point. To find out more about them, go to http://poaf.org/ and https://www.nationalcops.org/.

Jessica had these words of wisdom for those who are dealing with a life-threating injury:

- Faith is everything. Have faith in your marriage and in God to get you through the tough times.
- My marriage would have failed without faith and our commitment to each other and God.
- Be patient. The healing process can be long, tiring, and difficult.
- My favorite Scripture is this: "The LORD will fight for you; you must be quiet" Exodus 14:14 (HCSB).

Theresa's words of wisdom and hope are about enjoying life together, with no regrets.

- Teach your children to put God first, stay true to yourself, keep family close, and do what makes you happy.
- Remember, you love the man first. Then you can love the officer.
- Live with passion, love, and understanding because you never know what tomorrow brings.
- Never go to bed angry.
- Protect yourself. Do your finances together and make sure you take time to create a will.
- Begin developing relationships with others now. Be present and show up so your relationships can grow.
- You will never get over the loss. You are a survivor and must move forward.
- Don't do it on your own. Cling to good people. Allow yourself to grieve with family members, law enforcement friends, and Christian friends that bring you comfort. All of these "families" are very significant connections to have.

I have found encouragement, strength, and comfort in this Scripture. Joshua 1:9 says, "Be strong and courageous. Do not be afraid; do not be discouraged, for the LORD your God will be with you wherever you go."

BOLO 17

Blue Nation

Be on the lookout for the almost one million commissioned officers serving us across our nation. You will find them in a vast array of law enforcement departments, agencies, and positions. As spouses of a law enforcement officer, we are part of a unique, proud family of blue who love and support each other and these brave officers.

THE LAW ENFORCEMENT COMMUNITY is strong and diverse. We are part of an exceptionally large extended family that lives and works in every city and state of our great nation, from small-town USA to major metropolis. Our officers serve in federal agencies such as the U.S. Marshals, the FBI, and the DEA, just to name a few. They serve as well in the smallest of municipalities.

Officers are out there on duty, twenty-four hours a day, seven days a week, three hundred and sixty-five days a year in every capacity imaginable, including, in K-9 units, bike patrols, horse patrols, undercover, and special operations. There are so many different shift schedules and areas of law enforcement your spouse can serve in; and there is no telling where he may be or for how long.

Your officer might be called to serve on a special assignment for homeland security or one of the many other specialized assignments in the law enforcement world. He could be an honor guard or rise through the ranks in your local community police department and one day become Chief of Police.

You might also experience life with your LEO as a highway patrol officer, a motorcycle officer (also known as "motor jock"), or a detective for some or most of his career. He might choose to work the midnight shift for a lengthy period of time or work in the roughest part of your town. Or he may have no choice in what shift or assignment he serves in.

Robert, JoAnne's husband, who has been with his department for less than three years, recently went through a week-long training to become qualified as a bike officer. He also served as a lake patrol officer and has been through the SWAT training.

One officer I know of, Dick Hill at the Arlington Police Department, has been a motor jock for over forty years. That is an impressive career.

My husband served in many different capacities throughout his twenty-six year career with the Arlington Police Department.

Jay started his career as a patrol officer; he then was promoted to corporal as a field-training officer (FTO). While there, he received training as an accident investigator. He joined the tactical team and became a hostage negotiator.

Jay then was selected to the Criminal Investigation Division (CID) as an auto theft detective. As my earlier chapters detailed, Jay was transferred to the crimes against persons unit (CID), which included such offences, as robbery, aggravated assault, rape, and homicide. After a few years in CID, he promoted to sergeant and was assigned back to patrol.

Within three years he was transferred back into CID as a burglary sergeant. But within a year he was selected as the sergeant for the newly developed vice unit. After his service in the vice unit, he was chosen to serve as the sergeant for the school resource unit (SRO). Ultimately his last assignment, prior to retirement was back where he started his career, on patrol, as a sergeant.

Jay loved the variety of his career. These departmental moves kept his career fresh and exciting.

After retirement from the APD, he volunteered as a patrol officer, part-time for a small, neighboring community. He then tried civilian life for a short period of time but, no surprise to me or anyone else who knows him well, he went back into law enforcement. As of this time, for the past nine years Jay has served as a Court Security Officer (CSO) with the U.S. Marshals service, where his primary responsibility is to protect our federal judges.

When LEOWs see an officer on patrol who is working a sports event or concert, or who is protecting the rights of our country at a picket line, we feel a connection and instantly relate to them. When we hear of officers who are injured or lose their life in the line of duty, we feel a stronger connection to the grief of their families and communities. That connection is what I call the Blue Nation.

A few months ago, Jay and I attended an annual "Back the Blue" community event sponsored by the Arlington Police Foundation. This Foundation funds essential equipment and programs for the Arlington Police Department that are not included in the city budget. In addition, the Foundation provides financial assistance to the families of law enforcement officers killed in the line of duty.

Over five hundred citizens, officers, and retirees came together at the Foundation's event to support the men and women in blue. Attendees wore shades of blue to honor our Blue Nation. The Foundation honored legendary Motor Officer Corporal Dick Hill, #279, for his forty-three years of service with APD. This long-serving officer is a football Hall of Honor graduate of the University of Texas at Arlington (UTA) and played professionally with the Chicago Bears and Philadelphia Eagles. In addition, he was one of the original members of the APD SWAT team and Officer of the Year in 1996.

The Foundation also honored APD Chaplain Harold Elliott, who has been serving as Chaplain since 1975, pastored at five churches, produced two films, and has authored two books to date. He was honored for his forty-two years of service.

Jay and I had a wonderful time at the Foundation's event and were thrilled to be the highest bidder for a weekend at a cabin in the Texas Hill Country, just one of the numerous items offered at the silent auction. We also enjoyed hearing a local news anchor who was the keynote speaker. She mentioned that one of her family members is an officer serving in a nearby city. After her speech, a video explained how the funds raised are distributed and named the Foundation programs that have been supported over the past twelve months.

This video ended with pictures of the following APD officers and displayed their End of Watch (EOW) date: James Johnson, EOW November 23, 1930; Gary Harl, EOW July 16, 1975; Terry Lewis, EOW October 9, 1992; Jerry Crocker, EOW October 9, 1992; Craig Hanking, EOW August 3, 1994; Joseph "Joey" Cushman, EOW June 7, 2001; Craig Story, EOW January 13, 2010; and Jillian Smith, EOW December 28, 2010.

Families of the eight fallen officers in the video were invited guests at this "Back the Blue" event. They were recognized and honored during this portion of the program. As I watched the video and saw the family members stand for recognition of their sacrifices, I felt the sense of community with them and began to reminisce.

My mind took me back to a time many years ago when two of these fallen officers and their families touched my heart, so much so they will forever be remembered in my poem, "Coffee and Donuts: a Tribute to My Husband." Their touching storyline is included in this book in BOLO 8: My Daddy Is a Real Policeman.

Many family members of these two officers also were present. When I looked over to the tables filled with their loved ones, I felt the need to reach out to one of them, Jeri Lyn, the daughter of Jerry J. Crocker.

I privately asked her if she would consider an interview over lunch sometime soon and she agreed. We were able to meet at one of my favorite Tex-Mex restaurants for chips, chili con queso, and sizzling Tex-Mex style spicy fajitas, which is a favorite among most Texans.

Jeri Lyn's story shared that day shows a remarkable demonstration of our Blue Nation taking care of our own, being there for the healing process and beyond. In 1992 Jeri Lyn's father changed career paths from an interim Baptist pastor for several churches in neighboring towns to pursue his dream of becoming a police officer. Sadly, his dream was just a brief six weeks with the Arlington Police Department before his EOW, October 9, 1992. The circumstances of his death point out one of the many dangerous situations officers face in the call of duty.

Officers Terry Lynn Lewis and Jerry J. Crocker had just finished a call assisting the victim of a hit-and-run accident when a driver who was later determined to be intoxicated broadsided their patrol car. This tragedy was also a hit-and-run accident. The suspect eventually was arrested. He was convicted of intoxicated manslaughter and sentenced to five years in prison and then deported to his native country.

Jeri Lyn was only fifteen years old when the drunk driver killed her father and his partner. She told me, "I will never forget that fateful Friday night, October 9, 1992. It was 11:58 p.m., and I was at home in my room with the door closed. I took notice when the doorbell and phone rang simultaneously. Just moments later, I heard my mother's cry and I instantly knew."

Jeri Lyn continued her story, telling how her heart sank when she heard her mother's scream. "Somehow I knew my father was dead and remarkably how he died."

Not long after the doorbell rang, her grandmother came into her room to tell her the sad news. But before she could say anything, Jeri Lyn spoke up.

"Dad was killed by a drunk driver, wasn't he?"

Her grandmother consoled her as her fears were confirmed.

"How did I know?" she said. "It just made sense to me because one of the last things my father said was, 'The only reason I wouldn't see you again is if I were killed by a drunk driver.'"

Interestingly, Jeri Lyn told me that her father's partner, Terry Lewis, had recently had a conversation with his wife and said to her, "We need to take care of a few things just in case I go to work and get killed by a drunk driver."

Although Jeri Lyn knew instantly how her father died, she still had to see with her own eyes the patrol car her father and his partner were killed in. Her strong will and determination eventually persuaded her mother to say yes to this request. The Sunday after the accident, an off-duty officer drove her to the wrecker yard where the patrol unit had been taken.

"I remember looking at the passenger seat where my father would have been, and then I glanced over to the driver's side. Medical IV bags were still hanging from when the paramedics tried their best to save the lives of my dad and Terry. Although it was an emotional moment, sad and surreal, I was glad my mom allowed me to go."

Jeri Lyn then shared with me how her family scheduled two memorial services for her father, one local and one in Madisonville, Texas. Her dad's family was originally from Madisonville, a small town about an hour and a half away from Arlington. This quaint, historical town with a population just slightly over four thousand residents was named after President James Madison. Greyhound bus service offered two busses to drive the Crocker family, officers, and friends to and from Madisonville for that service.

"Hundreds of officers attended both services. The churches were overflowed with officers, family, and friends. The number was especially noticeable in the small church in Madisonville. Church members had prepared enough food for the immediate family right after the service, but my grandmother was prepared to serve the hundreds of officers who attended my dad's funeral. She invited them to her home for a bite to eat before driving back home to Arlington." Jeri Lyn chuckled and then added, "It reminded me of the bread and fish story in the Bible, Matthew 14:17–20."

The Blue Nation love and support for these families did not stop after the services. Arlington Police officers continued to reach out to the Crocker and Lewis family members during this troubling time and offered assistance to help with the healing process.

All this kindness and "blue love" made a very big impact on 15-year-old Jeri Lyn. A short six weeks after the loss of her father, she asked her mother repeatedly if she could go on a "ride out" with a police officer, indicating that she wanted to experience firsthand what it was like to ride in a patrol car. Reluctantly, as you can imagine, her mother signed the release form for Jeri Lyn to "ride out." Afterward and from time-to-time, officers would go to Jeri Lyn's school, pick her up in a patrol car, and take her to play video games.

"Officers even showed up to my sister's graduation, and Officer Pilcher walked me down the aisle in place of my dad years later when I got married," she told me.

As Jeri Lyn and I finished the satisfying Tex-Mex lunch, our conversation moved to the topic of how one life could impact so many others. Because officers from the APD had a huge influence in her life, she began making a difference in the lives of others. The death of her father had an effect in my life as well (see BOLO 8: My Daddy Is a Real Policeman).

Soon after her father's death and still just a teenager herself, Jeri Lyn began her ministry to spread the word against drinking and driving, especially to other teenagers. Her grassroots effort presented itself in speaking engagements, specifically around the time of proms and graduations. Jeri Lyn would travel to the surrounding communities, telling her story in hope of making a difference and saving lives.

Like her father, Jeri Lyn has a servant heart. At the early age of nineteen, just four years after the death of her father, she became a dispatcher with the Arlington Police Department and has been serving APD for over twenty years.

"I'm at peace," Jeri Lyn said to me. "I have forgiven the man that killed my dad."

Jeri Lyn's story is an example of our Blue Nation looking out for each other. In her father's absence, officers stepped in for the Crocker family. It is a wonderful story of what our law enforcement family is capable of doing.

While I continued my research, it didn't take long for me to think of PJ Brock. She is an amazing woman who has served as a law enforcement officer for over forty years, which includes her time with the US Air Force and twenty-seven years with the APD. She is an excellent example of someone who understands and dedicates herself to our Blue Nation. In a nutshell, she shows up!

PJ is well-known in our local Blue Nation and to many people in the law enforcement world. She has been seen volunteering inside and outside our community. I've seen her standing side by side with our local chaplain, helping those in need. Also, during the Texas Peace Officer Memorial in Austin, Texas, I saw her working tirelessly to help make sure all the chairs were set up so the event would go smoothly. At one moment, she even had her picture taken alongside the Governor of Texas.

PJ's behavior is selfless, authentic, humble, and a true testament to what Blue Nation is all about. Among her many other activities, she regularly attends the annual National Police Week in Washington, DC. Her husband, Mark Price, is by her side, supporting all her efforts.

In my interview with PJ, I asked her what Blue Nation meant to her.

"Well, we support each other. There are also people in our communities who are supporters of us, the first responders. These supporters take care of us, who take care of them."

I remember a time in my life when PJ was there for me. In the BOLO 10: "Altered" Egos, I referenced a time in my life when I broke both my ankles by stepping directly into a curbside street gutter in Austin, Texas. This accident happened during the processional at the Texas Peace Officers Memorial event. Once the ambulance came and whisked me off to the hospital, where the doctor assessed the damage and determined both ankles were broken, Jay had to leave me behind to retrieve our van.

While he was riding his motorcycle back to our hometown, PJ volunteered to come and sit with me. She kept me calm and kept Jay up-to-date on my condition. She also secured with a family in

Austin who would have allowed Jay to stay at their place should we be delayed in Austin for a while. Until then, I didn't even know her.

Recently, not long after my conversation with PJ, I saw a Facebook newsfeed that caught my attention. It was a live video of Deputy Constable Bryan Woodard. He was attending the funeral of Dallas Police Officer Rogelio Santander, EOW April 25, 2018.

In this video Bryan said, "This is what 'blue love' looks like. A sea of squad units ... all ages, all races, all colors, all sizes, all nationalities, all departments, constables, sheriffs, police officers, marshals, troopers. Every police department and law enforcement agency you can think of, even out-of-towners. We are one blue family, and that is why I am proud and honored to serve on the blue team."

I believe PJ's and Bryan's descriptions of our Blue Nation are spot on and we should be proud to be part of this "one blue family."

As a spouse of a law enforcement officer, likewise, we have a unique opportunity to connect with others locally and nationally through personal acts of service, events, and social media. I've noticed on social media that LEO wives discuss challenges on many issues. Topics range from "How do you wash your LEO's uniform?" to non-LEO related ones such as "How do you handle raising a four-year-old?" These women send love and prayers when exciting news such as a wedding or the birth of a child happens and, sadly, when tragedy strikes.

Being an active member in our Blue Nation on social media comes with a cost for us personally. We see, hear, and mourn in real time the concerns, injuries, and loss of our nation's officers, which on average happens about every other day. Our attempts to honor these shared concerns can hinder our ability to overcome some of the fears and anxiety associated with grief and loss. Without being insensitive to our Blue Nation's concerns, we must also protect our hearts.

Co-authors, David Kessler and Elisabeth Kübler-Ross in their books *Life Lessons* and *On Grief and Grieving* outline and describe the feelings and emotions of the five stages of grief—denial, anger, bargaining, depression and acceptance.

As a member of our Blue Nation, we might not realize we are suffering with grief, yet find ourselves in a continual struggle with one or more of the five stages.

If you are struggling with the villain or grief, I encourage you to consider limiting your use of social media.

The LEOW and LEO social media sites do their best to honor officers who are severely injured or lose their lives in the line of duty. It is important to do this, as the sites offer timely information in our Blue Nation. However, seeing and hearing about these injuries and losses weekly, daily, or sometimes twice a day can be crippling.

Day-to-day reminders of suffering and loss are not healthy for our well-being. I have read about women who suffer from anxiety so severely that they are sometimes sent home from work. Others say they are so worried about their husband's welfare that they beg them to quit. Some jump on the train of fear and frustration, which raises anxiety and sometimes anger toward these conversations on newsfeeds; thus, the cycle continues.

With that said, consider what your day would look like if you limited the social chatter of negativity and sorrow available daily from our Blue Nation. What would your day look like if you chose to honor the losses, not as they happen in real time but on an a monthly, semi-annual, or even annual basis? How much healthier could your life be with your LEO if you intentionally separated yourself from the daily law enforcement news?

I remember a time not long after Jay became a sergeant when I turned on the local news to catch up on current events. To my surprise, the news anchor was interviewing Jay, *aka* Sergeant Gus, about some tragic event. At that moment, I remember my heart beginning to race and I felt the villain surfacing. It wasn't the first time I'd seen him on the news, but that day it bothered me.

Maybe it was the reason he was being interviewed, which today I can't recall. I do know that during this time in Jay's career (late seventies and early eighties), the number of national LEO fatalities was significantly high. It was hovering around two hundred, which is staggering! Statistics also showed the use of firearms was the number one reason for loss of life and auto accidents a close second.

That day I quickly recognized I didn't have the time or the desire to fill my mind with the drama of his job. I thought to myself, *Vicki, seriously?* Then I laughed at myself as I said out loud, "Insanity is doing the same thing over and over and expecting different results." At that moment, I put on my imaginary bulletproof vest to give me the confidence and strength, and then I made the difficult decision to turn off the news.

When Jay arrived home, we talked about my decision to limit my news to once a week, which later became once every two weeks or longer. I didn't miss seeing and hearing about tragedy locally and nationally. I noticed my days were less stressful and frustrating. Eventually I told Jay that if there was something newsworthy, he could let me know. This simple change in my life was freeing. I felt the burden lifted. I was no longer paralyzed by current events. The villain kept its distance.

Debriefing

PJ's, Bryan's, and Jeri Lyn's stories are heartwarming and a tribute to the unconditional love of our Blue Nation. Stories like theirs continue to happen across our nation, and it is wonderful to know as well as comforting to know our Blue Nation has each other's "six," which means "their back."

In the Introduction of this book, I told about a heart-to-heart talk with a young new police wife, JoAnne. Her husband was a rookie at the time of our conversation, and she was fearful for her husband because of an incident that took place on the day he was "cut loose, riding solo" as an officer.

I asked JoAnne three years later how she is coping with the loss of officers in our Blue Nation. She told me, "I am doing okay. I'm learning how much I can handle and what triggers my fears to surface. I choose to 'hide' a lot of social media posts because I know if I dig deep into these posts and read all the comments, it would not be healthy for me. I have a family to raise, and I want my mind to be at peace so my focus is on our children, not the fears about the what-if's of my husband's job."

I love some of the statements JoAnne made, especially when she said, "I want my mind to be at peace." I hope you too see the value of finding the peace in your day and "turn off" what triggers your worry and fear.

There are many ways to serve our Blue Nation and become connected in positive ways. As mentioned earlier in this book, I started a Bible study in our area for law enforcement officers wives. When we connected for the first time, none of us knew each other; however, we knew all of us needed each other.

Currently four different departments are represented in our Bible study. Some husbands are rookies; others are seasoned officers, supervisors, motor officers, patrol, detectives, undercover, and retirees. We pray for and lean on each other for the good times and challenging times. Now we can't imagine our lives without our LEOW prayer warriors.

What can you do? What do you feel you need to do right now?

Bullet Points

Here are questions and thoughts to consider as you think about what Blue Nation means to you.

- What are your department and community doing to show their support to "back the blue"?
- Is there an organization hosting events to raise money for goods and services for law enforcement officers or first responders in your area? If so, great. If not, maybe you could organize something small that would grow over time. The Arlington Police Foundation's first annual Back the Blue

event started small and has grown to become an event our community looks forward to.

- How could your day be filled with peace, knowing you are a part of this Blue Nation? Consider this Bible verse: "Grace and peace be yours in abundance through the knowledge of God and of Jesus our Lord" (2 Peter 1:2).
- Would it be helpful for you and your loved ones if you began to phase out the overload of information of the daily news locally, nationally, and in our own Blue Nation? There are a lot of news options and social media sites available, so choose wisely.
- As a LEOW Blue Nation member, you can offer healthy support and coping skills to others. Many wives are suffering and paralyzed by the villain. Compassion and understanding go a long way. How are you contributing healthy support to others?
- Do you need support right now? Are you struggling with one of the five stages of grief? Possibly anger or depression? If so, consider doing more research on how to recognize and understand grief. Find a way to move towards a sense of peace, or acceptance. Some churches offer grief counseling or reach out to a professional.
- Compassion and understanding go a long way.
- Do you know there is a National Police Week in Washington, DC, held each year during the week in which May 15 falls? Consider attending at least once.
- Our city and state offer annual events during the month of May to honor the loss of our fallen officers. Does your city and state do the same?
- Ecclesiastes 3:4 says there is "a time to weep and a time to laugh, a time to mourn and a time to dance."
- Join an organization that helps other LEO families. Shield a Badge with a Prayer, for example, is a wonderful ministry that was started in my area by the Henz family. Tim Henz said, "It is free to everyone. You can pray individually or with others for officers daily. Our program is easy to get started and we

are here to help you." Go to the website to find out how to get started (http://www.shield-a-badge.org/).

- Look into other organizations that offer Christian support. Fellowship of Christian Peace Officers–USA has been around for a long time (http://www.fcpo.org/).
- Consider joining or starting a police wives organization in your community.
- Get to know the chaplain of your local police department.
- Many departments offer peer support groups such as Fraternal Order of Police (F.O.P.), which is national with local chapters (https://www.fop.net/).
- C.O.P.S. (Concerns of Police Survivors) is another wonderful national organization, which was also mentioned in BOLO 16 Sacrifices. "C.O.P.S. is the backbone of our Blue Nation," says PJ Brock. "It offers support to families, the children, and coworkers." This organization has local chapters in many cities across the nation. What started with 110 individuals in 1984 has grown to 47,000 survivors (https://www.concernsofpolicesurvivors.org/).
- Look into P.O.A.F. (Peace Officers Angel Foundation). Its mission is to offer emotional and short-term financial assistance to officers in the state of Texas following a serious or life-changing injury. You may have an organization like this one in your state (https://poaf.org/).
- The organization 10-7 Outdoors is a 501c3 nonprofit that provides hunting and fishing trips to the children of fallen officers across the country (*http://www.10-7outdoors.com/*).

Hebrews 10: 24-25 says, "and let us consider how we may spur one another on toward love and good deeds, not giving up meeting together, as some are in the habit of doing, but encouraging one another—and all the more as you see the Day approaching."

BOLO **18**

Youʼve Got This!

Be on the lookout for you to embody inner strength and courage. You are armed and ready. You have what you need to be independent, strong, and brave enough to conquer the villain and face down a gremlin when it appears. With an adequate amount of faith, coping skills, and your imaginary bulletproof vest that's now custom-fitted for your needs, you are ready to tackle the days ahead. You've got this!

M Y IMAGINARY BULLETPROOF VEST may look well-worn and tattered, but there are enough threads left to prepare me for the next part of my journey. In the distance, I can see Jay and me retiring someday. With this vision in mind, we've strategically placed two rocking chairs on the front porch in preparation of watching the beautiful Texas sunsets together.

As I look back on our journey as a law enforcement couple, I can say with confidence, "Our lifestyle became normal to us."

On my journey, I learned to embrace the uniqueness of our life together, and somehow it felt right and good. I learned to lean on my faith, and it has served me well. And I learned how to manage my family's day-to-day needs.

It became normal for me to be solo at many of our non-police events, and most of the time I didn't think much of it. We just did what we had to do based on his assignment and schedule.

Over time, I learned not to wake my sleeping cop and never to send the kids in to wake him. Instead it became normal for me to enter the bedroom, stay a certain distance away, make some noise, and call out his name until he woke up. Surprises were never good.

Even our laundry became normal. It overflowed with full loads of sweaty, dark T-shirts and bulletproof vest covers; for a few years, it included those stinky, smoky, undercover jeans and shirts.

Looking for police-related items in his pockets prior to sinking his clothes into the soapy water was a part of that normal. I'd look for his pocket-sized notepad with interesting scribbles such as license plate numbers and descriptions of suspicious persons. I'd dig deep into his pockets and sometimes find a bullet or two or one of his many knives that he'd tucked into his uniform pants, Tactical 5.11 brand, or everyday Wrangler brand jeans.

The back-to-back stories shared in *His Badge, My Story* are real-life, powerful, and most importantly, condensed to fit the time you take to read them. For that reason, you may be thinking, *Wow. Will I have to endure all these things?* If so, take heart. These experiences did not happen back to back or in a concentrated amount of time but throughout a long marriage and career in law enforcement. Also, Jay and I personally did not experience several of the stories shared by others.

Did I worry about Jay more than I should have? Maybe. But not as much as someone might think, especially after reading this book. I really did "get used to it." Still, a small amount of concern for him will forever linger in the back of my mind, and in my opinion that is perfectly normal.

Pleasant stories are encouraging; however, you may find yourself experiencing some of the not-so-pleasant situations recorded here. You may be wondering how well you will handle them. If so, let me assure you. Whatever experiences you encounter, whether commonplace or unique, just know that you *can* move from "will I ever get used to this?" to "I've got this!"

I have given these scenarios to help you better understand your spouse's job, and I have stressed the importance of understanding *him*, the man behind his badge. You have read about communication challenges, learned a variety of coping skills, and been debriefed with suggestions to help you find the strength and courage it may take to make it through whatever *you* actually experience.

You are a strong woman or will become one on your journey. Embrace it and enjoy this roller-coaster ride. I believe you will find your normal, just like we did. And with a thrifty budget and a modest lifestyle, you'll have a decent life together!

What will your story become over the years because of his badge? How many gremlins will come and go? How many times in his career will you fight the villain? How many bullets will you accidentally run through the washer?

With the demands of his job and unpredictable schedule, how many times will you feel the need to adjust your work or social calendar to make both of your lives more manageable?

Most importantly, what exciting stories will you have to share when you near the end of your journey? One thing I know for sure, your real-life stories will never be boring or mundane. You might even consider starting a journal of your own stories right now.

Debriefing

Thank you for allowing me to share *my* story with you because of *his* badge. I hope you have gained insights, coping skills, and confidence to tackle the challenges as well as the dangers he may face.

And now, a special thank you to the couple from the nonmandatory but highly recommended meeting for police spouses. Their words of wisdom have now been passed on to you, the next generation.

Please extend my thanks and Jay's to your law enforcement officer for their service. And thank you for supporting them through their calling to protect and serve.

May God bless you and your family in the coming years. Jay and I pray for your spouse's safety and your strength and courage to enjoy a healthy, long, and faith-filled life together.

You've got this!

Bullet Points

I would love to connect with you and hear your stories. Here are ways for you to connect with me.

- Visit my website: *https://leowinsight.com/*
- Follow me on social media
- Facebook: *@LEOWInsight*
- Instagram: *https://www.instagram.com/leowinsight/?hl=e*
- Twitter: *LEOW Insight (@InsightLeow)*
- As a certified Christian life coach, I specialize in helping wives and loved ones on their journey with their law enforcement officer.
- If you are looking for dynamic speakers, visit our website to schedule a speaking engagement. Jay and I would love to come to your community and share *my story* because of *his badge.*

2 Corinthians 3:4 "Such confidence we have through Christ before God"

NOTES

BOLO 2: In Pursuit of Love and Happiness
Page 13: *"Sometimes the smallest"*: *https://www.goodreads.com/ quotes/8401191-sometimes-the-smallest-step-in-the-right-direction-ends-up*

BOLO 3: The Villain aka Worry and Fear
Page 18: "Worry" *https://www.google.com/search?ei=EhKIW4m 0IYTcsAXBlLTIBw&q=definition+for+worry*
Page 18: "Fear" *https://www.dictionary.com/browse/fear*

BOLO 4: Answering the Call
Page 25: *"Our souls are"*: *https://www.becomingminimalist.com/ harold-kushner-on-meaning/*
Page 25: "The Arlington Police Department's vision statement": *http://www.arlington-tx.gov/police/vision-values-goals/*
Page 26: "The Arlington Police Department's core values": *http:// www.arlington-tx.gov/police/vision-values-goals/*
Page 30: "The APD's mission": *http://www.arlington-tx.gov/police/ vision-values-goals/*
Page 33: "If you ever get": Cops and Donuts, Clare City, Michigan *https://copsdoughnuts.com/*

Page 33: "There is another one named": Cops and Donuts, Gaylord, Michigan *https://copsdoughnuts.com/*
Page 33: "an organization that offers Christian": Fellowship of Christian Peace Officers–USA *http://www.fcpo.org/*
Page 33: "Shield a Badge with a Prayer": *www.shield-a-badge.org/*
Page 33: "The Peacekeepers": by Michael Dye, based on *The Peacekeepers* (Advantage Inspirational, 2005).
Page 33: "A good book": Michael Catt and Steven and Alex Kendrick, *Honor Begins at Home* (Lifeway Press, 2011).

BOLO 7: Blue Christmas
Page 52: "The cbsnews.com site": *cbsnews.com/news/james-bigby-texas-inmate-to-be-executed-in-1987-slayings-of-man-infant/* March 13, 2017, 6:16 PM.
Page 52: "He wanted to 'kill a bunch of people'": *The Fort Worth Star Telegram* from the article by Nancy Visser and Ted Cilwick, 1987, "Slaying motives a puzzle."

BOLO 9: "Do" Process
Page 72: "meaning they think they can handle anything" *http://www.nytimes.com/1991/11/17/nyregion/fighting-the-john-wayne-syndrome.html*

BOLO 11: Gremlins aka Pitfalls
Page 99: *"Police officers are accustomed"*: Beth Sanborn, <u>*Law*</u> *and Order Magazine,* September 2014 *http://www.hendonpub.com/law_and_order/articles/2014/09/saving_police_marriages*
Page 100: *"Being the wife of"*: Melissa Littles, *http://www.thepolicewifelifeblog.com/blog/selfish-is-not-an-option-the-police-wife-life*

BOLO 13: The Spice aka (Vice) of Life

Page 116: "I know what I want to be when I grow up": Allan Saxe, *Arlington Citizen Journal*, "If somebody must do vice patrol" Thursday, September 26, 1991 by Allan Saxe.

Page 116: "Arlington police arrested fifteen men": "Division raid nets 15 arrests men are charged with prostitution." July 25, 1993, *Fort Worth Star Telegram*.

Page 116: "Adult tanning salons raided" "Adult tanning salons raided; 2 managers, 5 workers arrested". By Kristin Sullivan October 20, 1993, *Fort Worth Star Telegram*.

Page 116: "A woman unknowingly takes a job": *The Client List*, aired on Lifetime Network, July 19, 2010, *https://www.google.com/search?q=the+client+list+movie*

BOLO 14: Unsolved, Unsettled

Page 124: "Money is a good motive": Detective Gustafson quoted in *D Magazine http://www.dmagazine.com/publications/d-magazine/1989/august/t-h-e-wax-museum-murder-mystery/*

Page 124: "*Unsolved Mysteries*": *https://unsolved.com/gallery/patsy-wright/*

BOLO 15: Communication Complexities

Page 140: Author and speaker Andy Stanley: *iMarriage* Multnomah Publishers

Page 140: "Time and talk are always a winning combination": Drs. Les and Leslie Parrott, *Love Talk* (Duluth, GA: INJOY, Inc. 2004), Communication 101: Brushing Up on the Basics. "Making Time for Talk," page 40-41

Page 140: "Attending … is the word communication specialists": Parrott, "Attending Skills," page 43

Page 142: Chris Kyle Frog Foundation offers retreats *https://www. chriskylefrogfoundation.org/*

Page 142: Bless the Badge offers "Tactical Relationship Training" *https://blessthebadge.org/*

Page 142: "Blue marriage offers" Blue Marriage: *https://www.blue marriage.com/Scott and Leah Silverii:*

BOLO 16: Sacrifices

Page 145: "There is something you should know": *Blue Bloods* quote, episode September 27, 2017, Tom Selleck (character, Frank Reagan).

Page 146: "death of an officer": National Law Enforcement Officers Memorial Fund (NLEOMF) *http://www.nleomf.com/*

Page 148: "On December 28, 2010": Jillian Smith, *http://dfw.cbslocal. com/2010/12/28/police-officer-two-others-killed-in-arlington-shooting/*

Page 151: "*Maria was a volunteer*": C.O.P.S. organization *https:// www.nationalcops.org/*

Page 152: "In 2012, she founded": P.O.A.F. (Peace Officers Angel Foundation) *https://poaf.org/*

Page 155: "Because of his personal sacrifice": LET (Law Enforcement Today) *https://www.lawenforcementtoday.com/*

BOLO 17: Blue Nation

Page 160: "The Foundation honored legendary Motor Officer Corporal Dick Hill, #279": Arlington Police Foundation, 2018, Back the Blue Program, *http://arlingtonpolicefoundation.org/*

Page 161: "APD Chaplain Harold Elliott, who has been serving as Chaplain since 1975": Arlington Police Foundation, 2018, Back the Blue Program, *http://arlingtonpolicefoundation.org/*

Page 166: "This is what blue love looks like": Bryan Woodard, *https://www.facebook.com/BryanDWoodard/ videos/1862539727199895/*

Page 166: Co-authors, David Kessler and Elisabeth Kübler-Ross in their books *Life Lessons* and *On Grief and Grieving*: *https://grief. com/the-five-stages-of-grief/*

Page 169: "Arlington Police Foundation": *http://arlingtonpolice foundation.org/*

Page 170: "There's a National Police Week": *http://www.nleomf.org/ programs/policeweek/*

Page 170: "Shield a Badge with a Prayer": *http://www.shield-a-badge.org/*

Page171: "Fellowship of Christian Peace Officers–USA": *https:// www.fcpo.org/*

ABOUT THE AUTHOR

AT THE AGE OF twenty-one, Vicki married the love of her life, Jay Gustafson. Two years later Jay answered the call to begin his lifelong career in law enforcement. Vicki became an entrepreneur. While pursuing their careers, they raised three children and are now the proud grandparents of five beautiful grandchildren.

While her children were young, Vicki volunteered at the children's schools, was active in their church and participated in leadership positions.

For over forty years, Jay and Vicki have enjoyed their "date nights" at the ballpark, watching their favorite team, the Texas Rangers, and listening to those two famous words in baseball, "Play Ball!" In her spare time Vicki enjoys relaxing in the sunshine and writing. She is also a published poet.

Vicki's family is precious to her, and she loves sharing her family traditions with the next generation. She finds reasons to gather the family together, especially for birthday and holiday celebrations. If you visit her home during these times, you will find Vicki, *aka* Grandma, in the kitchen with at least one of her grandkids by her side, standing on a stepstool and helping her "whip up" something special to make these celebrations memorable. Her two Westies will be at their feet, wagging fluffy white tails, all in the hopes someone will intentionally drop something yummy, which they always do.

Life as a law enforcement officers wife presented Vicki with unexpected challenges. To manage it, she had to dig deep within herself, rely on her faith, and find the strength and courage to hold tight on the "roller coaster life" many law enforcement couples experience. Now, interestingly enough, her daughter's husband is a law enforcement officer. Knowing the challenges her daughter and husband might face has inspired Vicki to share her insights, experiences, and coping skills with them and the thousands of other law enforcement officers couples.

Vicki's entrepreneurial spirit led her to own three successful businesses. Most notably, she created and was the CEO of A Touch of Joy, Inc., At Westbury Manor, a wedding and catering business. Her desire to create and help fulfill brides' dream weddings and receptions made her a frontrunner in that industry for over a decade. To satisfy her desire to continue as an active parent and work with women, Vicki next pursued social selling. The past fourteen years as a cabi stylist. Over twenty years, she achieved countless awards in sales and leadership. These skills led her to be on leadership panels, keynote speaker and hold essential positions for many years. She also served on the board of the Women's Division at the Mansfield Chamber of Commerce.

Vicki has a special place in her heart for charities, especially those who serve women. She has participated in and coordinated events to raise funds for her community, breast cancer awareness, and the Heart of cabi Foundation, which fulfills the mission of encouraging and empowering women in need.

Her desire for leading and coaching women eventually guided her to attain certifications as a Christian Life Coach and a Professional Life Coach, CCLC/CPLC from Professional Christian Coaching and Counseling Academy—part of Anew University. She received professional training from coach Beth Jones-Schall of Spirit of Success, Sara Grady of Bevens Institute, and Robin Pou, Chief Advisor and Strategist of Robin Pou, Inc.

Vicki now specializes in helping law enforcement officer's wives with their life journey and unique challenges. As a guest speaker, she invites audiences into her story, keeping them captivated and engaged. Her insights touch hearts and offer a new and fresh perspective in the world of law enforcement. And now, because of his badge, she shares with these families what they might encounter. *His Badge, My Story* is her first book.